Breaking Free

No More Soul Suffocation

Zoe Anna Bell

Copyright © 2021 Zoe-Anna

Breaking Free–No More Soul Suffocation - Book cover design: Mala Letra Diseño Editorial.

All rights reserved. No part of this book may be used or reproduced by any means, graphic, electronic, or mechanical including photocopying, recording, taping or by any information storage retrieval system without the written permission of the author except in the case of brief quotations embodied in critical articles and reviews.

The information, ideas, and suggestions in this book are not intended as a substitute for professional medical advice. Before following any suggestions contained in this book, you should consult your personal physician. Neither the author nor the publisher shall be liable or responsible for any loss or damage allegedly arising as a consequence of your use or application of any information or suggestions in this book.

Because of the dynamic nature of the Internet, any web addresses or links contained in this book may have changed since the publication and may no longer be valid. The views expressed in this work are solely those of the author and do not necessarily reflect the views of the publisher, and the publisher hereby disclaims any responsibility for them.

The author of this book does not dispense medical advice or prescribe the use of any technique as a form of treatment for physical, emotional, or medical problems without the advice of a physician, either directly or indirectly. The intent of the author is only to offer information of a general nature to help you in our quest for emotional and spiritual well-being. In the event you use any information in this book for yourself, which is your constitutional right, the author and the publisher assume no responsibility for your actions.

Breaking Free – No more Soul Suffocation - Ms. Zoe Anna Bell

Book 1 of a trilogy book series: FREE WILDFLOWER CODES

Publication November 2021 RAW Publishing

ISBN: 978-0-6481776-2-3

Dedication

This book is dedicated to all those who feel stuck in a rut with a gnawing feeling that there is more to life. A society where many are held captive, be it by their body, mind or life circumstance with shame, guilt, fear and rage standing at the door.

This is for the souls who have spent a lifetime attempting to fit in, interchanging masks to feel normal or accepted. This is dedicated to every soul, so they too may find a way to express their raw essence of 'badassary' and break free of the bullshit (BS) opinions in society. This is for the weird and wild ones that choose to run with the wolves.

It is my pure intention to awaken, stir, and inspire You the reader to appreciate adversities, life challenges and pain as magical doorways of experience leading to unveil Your Soul mission. A path of soul remembrance through transmutation of inner healing. As you venture on your own inner journey be aware that Your Soul mission may begin to reveal the truth of You. This is explored in book 3, Soul Codes – Remembering Your Mission.

This book series is dedicated to my beautiful children, Jake and Charlie, divine gifts on loan from the Universe. May this give you a deeper insight into the sacredness of the feminine and why I am the way I am. Each challenge is a wise teacher and to trust in the power of imagination and dreaming.

Adversity is your greatest ally

Embrace all aspects of life, the joy, the suffering, the celebration and the sorrow. As each step is as vital as the next, and even in times of pain and loss there is an invitation to gaze deeper into the heart and Soul. Remember that faith and trust are your wings of free soul expansion and you are never alone. My love for you is unconditional, eternal and you are complete in every way. I am proud to be your Mum, guide and friend. xxx

This book series is for women and men that shame their bodies, their sensual desires and are afraid to honour and express their raw truth. May this guide each soul out of the darkness and shift perceived imperfections into the sweet perfections of the magnificent and beautiful You.

Your story holds messages, inner wisdom, the pieces of the puzzle.

I was blind, and now I see, I was deaf, and now I hear, I was numb, and now I feel.

To my Mum and Sister, thank you for walking alongside me until I was ready to spread my wings and soar into my greatest expansion. I always knew I would be a later bloomer and I never gave up dreaming.

To my niece, Arienne, blossoming into womanhood, may this series be a guide for you and other teenage girls that are seeking direction and the rites of passage into womanhood.

Each moment is an opportunity to awaken and break free of the illusion we are fed. Now, let us all rise and re-claim the power within.

It is time to stop suffocating the soul and choose a path of breaking free. It is time to unleash this book, so others can be inspired from this path of the past. Life has been shifting so fast, moment to moment that it is now time to stop writing and allow this to inspire another's path.

Contents

FOUR WORDS xi

INTRODUCTION 1

CHAPTER 1: LIFE'S BLUEPRINT 9
This Mission 9
My Childhood 11
    A Perfect Lesson 44
Coming Home 77
    Loosing Myself 83

CHAPTER 2: FINDING MY VOICE 119
Voices In The Head 119
An Inner Voice of Wisdom 125

CHAPTER 3: THE HUMAN EXPERIENCE 131
Creative Forces Of The Mind 131
    Law of Abundance 132
    Words as S-Words 134

Discern in all choices.. 136

The Body Talks... 139

CHAPTER 4: WHO ARE YOU? 145

A Square Peg **145**

A Freaky Genius **149**

Primary Gifts 152

Secondary Gifts.. 157

Complementary Gifts... 161

CHAPTER 5: WHAT IS BLOCKING YOU?......................... 163

Unlocking Your Greatness? **163**

The Enemy Will Hide..**166**

Breaking The Chains.. 169

Intuitive messages... 172

CHAPTER 6: FREEDOM FROM SHAME 181

Feeling Trapped **181**

Energy and Attention..**186**

Breakout to breakthrough.. 187

Pay It Forward 192

CHAPTER 7: THE NAKED TRUTH 199
Peeling Back The Masks..................199
   Why do we create the masks? 200
   Faulty Wiring Patterns..................208

CHAPTER 8: THE PINK ELEPHANT 211
Fear Unpacked 211
   Do you fight?..................212
   Do you run? 213
   Do you freeze? 213
Moving Forward..................214
   re-cap and run down..................215
   Ownership with Honesty..................216
   Accountability with Action 216
   Ruthless Responsibility 217

CONCLUSION 223
BIBLIOGRAPHICAL RESOURCES..................235
ACKNOWLEDGMENTS..................237
ABOUT THE AUTHOR..................239
CONNECT WITH ZOE..................241

FOUR WORDS

When you have shifted and changed as much as I have and let go of the story you are about to read, it is important to add a fresh perspective of who I am now and not where I came from. A way to weave my essence beyond the gauntlet of trauma and inner suffering I was blessed to experience as a path to Soul Remembrance.

I asked 22 men and women that know my Soul and in receiving what they wrote my heart bowed in deep humility. Below are 11, the remaining 11 are in *Wildflower -Reclaiming a Sacred Place*. To my Mum, I love you infinitely beyond how we each see the world. This is my story.

The question was.

'Can you give a Synopsis of Zoe in 4 words.'

Tone Mellard: Tiny Container – Gigantic Spirit

Meli-Jane Knight: - Diversely Life-Experienced – Introspective - Adventurous

Kym-Louise Heyman: Courageous – Magnetic – Knowing - Nurturing

Katrina Geyer: Powerful – Juicy – Unapologetic – Candid

Anne Marie: Truth – Strength – Love – Beautiful

Amy Maree: Goddess – Freedom – Spirit Warrior

Wren Dubois: Independent – Daring – Spiritual – Fit

Danielle Alexandria: Fearless Warrior – Compassion – Way shower – Lightening

Melina MacDonald: Expansive – Risk Taker – Alien (Visitor) – Wild Spirit

Tanya Dan: Sublime – Sacred – Alchemist – Wild

Denby Sheather: Charismatic – Authentic – Pioneer – Grounded

I asked my two teenage boys to describe me in one word and this is their contribution.

Jake (14) – Truthful

Charlie (13) – Loving

The four most consistent words will be in *Soul Codes – Remembering Your Mission*.

INTRODUCTION

Welcome to Breaking Free – No More Soul Suffocation. I have had resistance with sharing the past, as it has no relevance in the now. Yet, I feel by sharing my past story others may be inspired to have the courage to break-free and transform events of raw vulnerability into finding inner freedom and have the courage to open the doorway of soul remembrance.

It is time to pay it forward.

Included herein are individuals that I respect, forgive and wish to protect their identity. The power of poetry revealed a gift to share my voice and heart expression. The purpose for any story is to learn the lesson and move on; I believe it is not for others to embellish within and I have no emotional attachment to any of it. Be inspired to be that change, as I believe there is something for everyone to learn; may this be your own unique journey back to you. It is my intention to shine love and light onto the darkest aspects that souls hide from, be it the abuser, the victim, the rescuer as we are all one. We each play each part, flipping to different roles in this game of life. We all deserve to be loved, as love and acceptance are unconditional. Self-forgiveness and compassion are vital. We are reflective mirrors, teachers and students of one another as we explore this crazy game called life. Each soul can break free of their insanity, as love is the way.

I am grateful for the lessons and I am blessed. My name is Zoe Anna and this is my story.

Some have known me as Becky Bell, and this is my story.

You can call me Zoe or simply Z.

I am allowing You into a deeper understanding of my adventures of waking up, as I believe others will resonate. For this, give yourself permission to open into who you are at your core, even if you are yet to know who that is. This will start to open the doorway back to the empowered, sensual, vibrant You, and allow You to express your wild spirit freely.

I know this is a book you have been drawn to, as in some shape or form you are curious to understand yourself, or maybe to understand more about my life. I have had the honour to work with many clients over the years, gaining golden insights from each colourful journey and what I have observed, is we are not so different. When you take off the masks and peel back the layers, we are all going through similar human challenges.

What I invite you to do is to trust your intuition, and as you digest what is within the book, remember to pause, *tune-in, check-in and feel.* If at any time you feel threatened or confronted remind yourself that all you need to do is to become curious about whatever comes up for you. Any inner reaction and emotional charge hold within it a deeper meaning awaiting your attention, acknowledgement and affection. This may involve being heard, held, or inner healing work. Have loving acceptance of where you are currently at, as this adventure is to be courageously honoured and respected.

My intention is to create a safe, open space to explore your unique journey of self-evaluation of where you are at now and begin to unravel what is keeping you stuck. Taking responsibility is a key to gaining personal freedom and an aspect of the (r)evolution of you. You never know what you will find out about yourself when you stay open to what comes up.

INTRODUCTION

Fear, shame and denial on the other hand, are the kinds of things that will keep you closed in fear and hiding. If you experience any resistance to your calling to be free, then keep exploring the depths within, as your soul holds the answers that your heart seeks.

I feel we are within an exciting spiritual evolution of self and sexual revolution, where there are more empowered choices and an invitation to become more curious, as we may have all lived many past lives as both man and woman.

Welcome to the three-part book series – Free Wildflower Codes. This first book *Breaking Free – No More Soul Suffocation*, is to reveal blocks in order to break free, so we can fearlessly dive in deeper with *Wildflower – Reclaiming a Sacred Place*, to honour the most vulnerable and sacred aspects of a woman. Yes, honouring the yoni to re-claim sovereignty of the womb space to reveal secrets and wisdom to unveil your unique *Soul Codes – Remembering Your Mission* the final book of the series, to remember your soul mission for humanity.

My mission is to cultivate shameless awareness in sensuality, free expression and inspire souls to let go of what is no longer serving or relevant within this present moment. It is time to view all aspects of your ever-morphing inter-changing personality with compassion, to let go of who you think you are and dissolve the veils of the *illusion.*

It is when you begin taking responsibility for everything that happens to you, that you gain the ability to tap into the fullness of you. If you start feeling confused or confronted, think of that as being an exciting place to be. This is the perfect place just before opening.

During the early stage of writing this book, many beautiful souls came forward offering their services, their bodies, and creative talents, so know that what is contained herein is both potent and powerful. This will start the ball rolling and begin to draw to you all that you desire. Who I was then, is not who I am choosing today.

Sexuality and sensuality are our wholeness. It is as normal as exploring the foods we love, how to move our body, remember our animal body, and re-connect with our natural environment. For many of us, we may have been shamed by experimenting through touch when we were small; and for some as toddlers exploring touch with other toddlers. Sensuality is also the gateway to unlock the creative spirited self. The life-force energy of your body is sensual in nature.

It was time to step up and speak about the 'unspeakable' and to make some noise so others can see what is keeping them trapped. To become free from what they are led to believe and to shift adversity and illness into the greatest gifts. It is time to lead others, so they can take back their power. It was a week before beginning the re-write and splitting the original book, that I went live on social media, and shamelessly announced that I was virus free. As you read about my journey, I created my own worst nightmare, so that I could heal myself from the inside out.

I am grateful for the teachers, that they were perfectly good and perfectly bad depending on my needs at the end of the day. From a greater perspective as a multi-dimensional being, I do not see good or bad. The men and women who treated me like crap were providing the contrast, and from the suffering, new awareness to rise above and begin to honour the light that had been forgotten within myself. To feel, own and embrace the darkness with loving kindness, in order to love me back into wholeness. The self-realisation was that my experience was directly reflecting exactly how I was not valuing myself. I was abusing my own soul, specifically my own inner child, I was ignoring her cries.

INTRODUCTION

Everyday my heart opens and expands, we are limitless and to trust in the process unfolding is freedom; each new day, breath, moment is a gift waiting to be opened and explored. Life is a never-ending journey to know thy self. Get ready to think outside the box and be prepared to stop jumping through other people's hoops/demands. It is time to follow your own truth and lifelong dreams. Each day I let go even more and free fall forward, into a new adventure. I still meet challenges for my inner growth, as there is no fucking hiding from the realness of life.

"You have to lose yourself, to find yourself, No one else can put you together, It is an inside job."

– Zoe Anna

It is time to freely express with confidence what you desire and to start exploring this great adventure of who you came here to be. It's your basic human right to be living and thriving as a human being. Every aspect of who you are as a spiritual being living a human experience in a body here on beautiful planet Earth. This is the magical journey back to you, unveiling the beautiful you. It is time to be fearless and move forward with your life. Get ready to create a deeper level of intimacy with yourself, and then with others.

"Suffering is part of our training program for becoming wise." Ram Dass

There will be people that come into your life, soul messengers, connections who come in as fast as they leave. It is never about the other person; it all comes back to you. They are beautiful mirrors to assist you in letting go, healing and remembering to love deeper aspects of yourself once forgotten.

MY MEMOIR

Chapter 1: Life's Blueprint

> *"Suffering is created from resistance to our incarnation."*
>
> – Ram Dass

This Mission

As Star seeds and Souls, we chose to come back to get it right this lifetime. To take responsibility and be the cause of our life. To shift the impact, we have on our environment, and bring humanity to a place of peace and synergy. With awareness of waking-up, each soul plays an integral part in resetting and restoring the balance for Mother Earth. Many are already uniting as tribes, all in preparation for a greater plan in 2020 and beyond. Much is being discovered within the 'unseen' and 'magical realms', as life is shifting so fast, who knows where we will be when this is being read.

During direct communication with the angelic realm I was told that I was birthed upon a prayer. Humanity had been crying out, for radical change, and yet even though they need what I have to offer, they may not necessarily want it. I know I am here to shift the balance and part of this global shift is to bring in sacred sensuality. The numbers 144,000 souls may mean something to you or have zero relevance.

It is time to heal the ocean of rage and sexual repression, which begins with self. Little did I know at the time that six months later I would be aligned with other powerful souls, and the upgrades that would follow continue to unravel and shift, as into early and now mid 2019, more is being revealed.

I am still learning, growing, evolving and I am far from perfect. The lessons perfect for growth, and inner healing to unleash the gifts of divine wisdom.

Through this transparency you have an opportunity to gain insight into what you can shift if you so choose. This may be different to your own beliefs; I am not here to challenge your beliefs as they are barriers to keeping you stuck in the story, of how it 'should' be. This is my opinion and at the end of the day the lessons are the same, no matter the diversity of beliefs. The greater the resistance, the greater the separation within.

Before you enter into my past story, ask yourself these questions.

- Do you care what happened to you?
- Do you feel trapped or tied to your past?
- Do you connect more with others in a group who share your past story?
- Do you wear and carry your story around with you?
- Does your story define you?

There is no right or wrong answer, view this as a barometer to gauge where you are at currently. I am not my story, and neither are you! The lessons are an opportunity to learn from, carve out, and shape you into who you came here to be. This is your soul destiny, and an aspect to your Soul Blueprint.

MY CHILDHOOD

Growing up in England and Wales of the UK, like many teenagers, I struggled with developing a healthy body image. As with many young girls/teens behind closed doors, I too thought there was something wrong with me. I felt different, especially when puberty kicked in at 10 years old. My body and I had to learn how to grow into one another. My experience was, what I saw, I hated.

"When we learn to love the skin and sin, we are in, we begin to see that sin was internally created."

— Zoe Anna

People that knew me in my youth have been shocked when they viewed more recent pictures of me. It is true what they say about beauty, as it happens on the inside by the way we see ourselves. Our thoughts impact the genetic coding of our biological DNA. I was funny and outgoing right up until we moved to England at 16 years old. A new school, I felt lost, the girls were bitchy as I connected more with boys. I struggled to fit in with the question, "Where do I belong?"

Like a chameleon taking on many different looks, re-creating who I thought I needed to be, in the attempt to fit into groups. I wanted to belong and fit in somewhere. Still, today in society nothing much has changed; we have the BS of social media selfies that have been photoshopped. Thinking I had to fit into a definition of normal, a perfect key of life lessons to embrace my weird. People still think I am weird, yet I love and embrace this as part of who I am.

This story and my life are like chapters in a book. Many doors are now closed never to be opened again, and like many, lessons rolled into one. I am grateful to still be connected to friends in Wales, bonds of deep friendships that forever run deep. Life growing up in Wales from the ages of 8-16, were the best and most fun years of my life, until now.

When writing this book, it was a challenge to sort life happenings into order as there were blacked out spots deep within my memory, specifically in the right-hand side of the brain. Perhaps this was a survival thing, so I did not go into complete mental and emotional shut-down from the intense trauma I experienced. It was not until September 2018 that the black spots would begin to find a way to fill with light during a birthing of inner seeing. This process is still unfolding. I am blessed with three of intuitive gifts, claircognizance (clear knowing), clairsentience (clear feeling) and clairaudience (clear hearing).

It has been soul-freeing to interweave raw and painful experiences into poem. There is no specific time frame; after all, time is the biggest illusion there is.

Many experiences are sensitive with dark aspects of story that needs to be heard. It is my pure intention to be a voice so others can relate and to be inspired to shift inside. I am passionate about empowering youth and each soul to express your truth no matter how dark. It is all beautiful as it is a soul free expression, and this is a gift. Each of our voices need to be heard, especially if you have had a flavour of powerlessness, hopelessness and worthlessness as part of your journey.

Let us continue with the story.

As a teenager and young adult, I was the whirlwind moving from drama to drama, accident to accident, and trauma to trauma. While achieving much in music and competitive sport, on the inside I was confused and sad. I was rebelling against different belief systems, and like many teenagers chose to go against the grain of my family, doing everything to disagree and be diversely different. Deep down, I was finding my own way of re-structuring my belief system and values. The dark years, post age 17, I began to reject creativity, music, art and movement, replacing them with destructive ways to numb out from the pain I was enduring.

Welcome to the karmic merry-go-round that keeps spinning round and round, bringing other similar events at accelerated speed, yet dressed up in a different way. Getting stuck here until the lesson was learnt. I was powerful at manifesting the unwanted, and there was force and fire behind it.

I knew there was a higher power, something greater than what I was being shown - a higher purpose. My family and their personal beliefs were the perfect contrast for what I was here to discover.

I love my family unconditionally, and it is vital for every teenager to form their own beliefs.

I rebelled at the idea of church and was raised with the belief that sex was within a committed relationship or marriage. As a curious teen I created shame around healthy sexual exploration.

I began to rebel pushing back against authority, as I felt suppression of healthy exploration and I pushed back against authority and rules. In the

1990's I felt drawn to hippies, free parties and paganism. It was the closest thing to being spiritual and we thrived on freedom. Looking back, it was the free spirit of dancing around fires, naked, free in nature and the ceremony that appealed to ancient warrior ancestral timelines, as a Viking. It was escapism away from my reality, maintaining my soul sanity from the rules of society and reliving past lives.

Growing up in a household with Mum, Dad, and an older Sister, I was curious and sexually inquisitive from a young age. My Dad was the local General Practitioner (GP) which may be why I was obsessed with the human body. I was intrigued by the difference between girls' and boys' genitalia and fascinated by sex from a noticeably young age.

I loved to dance, perform in plays, and would delight in twirling my body to music when we had guests. Dancing was a passion, a natural performer, my ego thrived on performing for an audience. As a baby I was fearless and curious, walking at eight months old, and being taught to jump out the cot by my clever 3-year-older sister. Apparently, I would swing in and out of my top floor bedroom window each morning, which to my mum's horror would be informed of this act by the neighbour; I was only three or four years old. My sister and I would play a game of push-me-down-the-stairs in the Ali Baba-esque washing basket, which included screaming with laughter, our parents oblivious to the adventures.

We had an abundance of highly charged energy, and mum steered us towards activities to burn off excess energy safely and supervised. I was fearless and ready to take on the world from an incredibly young age. A normal and favourite activity was to swing upside down on the clothesline; I was an active and happy cheeky monkey.

Often, I would be found curled up asleep snuggled up with our Labrador,

Gabble in his bed. These childhood memories remain, as I still love smelling dog's ears and the general smell of wet dogs.

My memory before the age of six is blurry, mostly recollected from pictures and stories from mum and my sister. So, where did it all start getting blurred?

The life that I knew was about to take a full 360-degree spin. Dad had met and fallen in love with someone else. Choosing another life, he followed his heart at the time. He had a three-year affair, living a double life until I was six years old. Growing up I put my dad on a pedestal and looked up to him as my hero. I created an imaginary dream inside my mind of how he would be, and yet he was trapped in a world of guilt, shame and blame. I felt disappointment after disappointment and longed for the daddy-daughter relationship.

I would push him away and he didn't know how to reach me in the times of crying out in silence. We were hurting on the inside and had lost our way to reach one another.

I tasted abandonment, disappointment and rejection. It would be a path to later reveal compassion, and forgiveness. The journey of abandonment within the mind of a child, remained with me up until I was 40 years old. At 6 years old there began deep numbing and emotional disconnection, my mum told me later on that I did not cry from the ages of 6 -12; I cried when our Dad told us he was leaving and that was it.

A separation from the once free spirited and playful child, my foundations of safety, stability as a family and belonging, shattered. Like many children in this situation I felt confused, hurt and wanting my parents to be back together. It was my one and only wish growing up.

This transferred into relationships with men. The hurt of abandonment and rejection started to manifest into deep-rooted anger and resentment.

This was to be a soul journey to heal at the age of forty-four years young, and see that abandonment and rejection was the theme of healing carried over multiple soul lifetimes. To learn a lesson that the only one that can ever abandon or reject me, is me. This was finally acknowledged in September 2018, during my Level 1 Training with Star Magic in Sedona facilitated by Jerry Sargeant - a Pleiadean brother from another mother. My soul journey was realigned and reset after exploring multiple past timelines. It was apparent that I had been brutally murdered in many timelines, at the hands of men. Through the facilitation of healing, my origin of this Star Realm was remembered.

It was three weeks before my dad left his physical body in December 2005 that I forgave him. My dad said sorry, we hugged, and we cried together and on that day our souls were set free. I feel blessed that I got to fly from Australia to England to complete this process. My sister never got the opportunity in person, as she was heavily pregnant. It was 30 minutes before he passed over that she gave birth to a beautiful baby girl, my beautiful niece and Goddaughter. As one soul departs another soul enters this universal plane, two soul adventures of new beginnings.

For years I thought that a part of our Dad's soul came back through my niece, until during a reading with a psychic medium, when another aspect was revealed. An aspect of his soul came back five months later.

The funny part is, I had mentioned to my son Jake before that he had been my father in another lifetime. Little did we realise it was this one.

LIFE'S BLUEPRINT

I learnt to forgive.

My Dad taught me to follow my heart and soul.

We learn about rules and get told so many times over and over that we forget to begin to get wired into questioning instinct and inner knowing. A child is a highly independent explorer with a mind of their own, and a powerful creator. A child leads with the heart and curious exploration. Yes, boundaries are vital, yet the strong will and free spirit of a child is precious. Over the years we each begin to adopt our caregiver's beliefs and forget who we are.

In school we are told to accept everything we are told as truth where questioning is discouraged. If we stand up as powerful creators then we were punished and given the label as stubborn, rebellious and insolent. We explored the body, playing strip shows and having disco dance-offs to the soundtrack of the movie Grease. I recall at school jumping up on the tables with one of the boys and we were busting out Greased Lightning fearlessly. On the flip side we were making go-carts and having street race challenges with the boys in our neighbourhood.

Where scuffed knees from climbing trees was the norm, scratches from building dens, and coming home covered in leaches from swimming in the river with stickler-back fish was the norm. Nature was our playground. As active and loving children we would pick flowers for the old lady who lived opposite us. She was a widow, and we picked her flowers from the garden and visited her with a fresh bouquet. She gave us biscuits, warm milk and a few silver coins. We felt rich, filling our pockets with chewing gum and 2 pence lollies, while we adventured on our push-bikes. Our young playful energy warmed her spirit and she marvelled in our joy drinking warm milk and munching down sweet cookies.

It was a magical win-win of sharing space and warm company. I played the cello from the age of 4-years old, practised ballet, gymnastics, and art/creativity/dance and drama was the norm with our mum. She was the most active and amazing mum I know.

We played, acting out sex, by making sounds and actions with our dolls. Lucky Action man and a collection of different looking and different coloured Cindy dolls. Cindy was the super cool doll of the 1970's before Barbie came along. No offence Barbie, but Cindy was ten times more feminine, curvaceous and real. It is very normal for children to play out sex games, the same way that children explore different sensations in their bodies. It is normal, and a part of healthy development as we learn through play. Sadly, this is where much shame and guilt had been created around sensuality.

We made mud pies, sand pies, ate worms and our days were filled with creative free play. It was the 1970's and I had a purple chopper bike with a flag on the back. Wow, it was a super-cool tomboy bike. We had pet rabbits, guinea pigs, and two dogs. Many rabbits died over the years; a dinner for the local cat, when they escaped from their cages, oops! Burial processions were normal, and we even had a wedding for the guinea pigs. My first boyfriend on my 5th birthday bought my first pet, 'Pinky', a guinea pig.

He also taught me how to tie my shoes laces whilst we shared kisses on his 5th birthday. I still have the locket of a girl and boy kissing he gave me for my 6th birthday.

My children a few years back came home and told me how they had the police come to the school and one of the things they addressed was inappropriate playing with dolls amongst a list of other things.

Many are unaware of the shame, guilt or blame around a healthy and normal self-exploration with dolls in play. As wrongdoing and shame created whilst young can then become the adult pervert peeping tom who must sneak to look at porn, or others, as they feel not worthy and guilty of their desires.

Fantasy is healthy. Just because someone fantasises about sex with an animal for example, does not make them a pervert. This may shock many, it is a fantasy. It is only when it becomes obsessional and brings direct harm, that it becomes an issue. The shame of having the fantasy is more likely to go onto a behaviour that is shameful and unhealthy for all parties. Allow children to explore their own bodies with their own hands and introduce that there are some things we do in private, with no shame attached! I have encouraged my boys to explore the sensations in their bodies and to instil self-love and self-acceptance of their beautiful bodies.

Pictures of me with family in my early years

I shared the story about exploratory play with my dolls to my children, so they could see that it is normal with healthy exploration. They said, "Mum that is weird stop it," we laughed. It is vital to keep the door open and never allow shame to be continued through generations. Be clear in your intention, give honest, direct and safe explanations, as when you lie you lose their trust and respect. Yes, there are also things that you can say is your personal business, as you are not their friend. As a parent you are a loving guide, until they are old enough to make their own choices. This requires ownership of actions and a willingness to be self-responsible. It is important to be free to explore through play and not make a big deal out of it. I like to keep it real with my kids. They are balanced, beautiful children and I want them to feel they can approach me on any topic and not carry around any blame, guilt and shame. After all, they have a mother who dares to be herself, and lives a life that does not conform with society and the outdated social paradigm.

Recreating Normal

Why can't we be one big happy family

Live in one home, together as one?

I like to swap my friends

Some better for soccer

Others better for super-hero games

And sometimes we all play

Together as great friends.

There is no fighting

No jealousy

No under siding

Life is quite simple

Everyone happy

Together as one.

We played a game

Like one happy family

Innocence of a little girl lost

A sweet five or six

Acting out the affair

LIFE'S BLUEPRINT

Even being caught in the act
Snuggling close
Her two boyfriends
Holding her close
Never to part.

A game to feel normal again
Never a struggle, a place for us all
Lying back on the grassy playground hill
Playing the game of one happy family
We innocently made sense of the mess
Clutching to hope and love in my heart
Needing to feel close
A child's loss
Whole world turned upside down
Oh, what a mess.

The man I adored, Daddy no longer there
Specific times now booked in for a special cuddle
Never available in a time of need
Tucking me into bed

BREAKING FREE

Stroking my hair with tender affection

The bedtime story read

Snuggles at bedtime

Never to be felt again.

My mummy falling apart

Confused and heart ripped open wide

Her whole world shattered

Flipped upon its side

Rebuilding from within the darkness within

Memories dissolved into emptiness

Dreams now lost, and visions dissolved

Responsibility to self and

Two children lost, seeking her guidance

Confusion of the new reality

Love matters of the broken heart.

She gave it her all and

Gave us the best

Relocation and a new adventure

Connected with nature

LIFE'S BLUEPRINT

Her love and energy, a passion for life
Her fight for life to be two parents in one
To never forget our inner spirits ever again.

You held the torch of hope
Guided with faith
God as your witness
Love in your heart
Until we could care for our own
Thank you, Mum
I found my way
I am finally home.

I started to masturbate young. When I asked my sister, she told me that she would start diddling while in our parent's bed when she was young too, at four years old; and they only tried to distract her, so there was never any shame around it.

As a family, before the separation we had two overseas holidays each year. Summer was going to France camping at the beach, and in Winter to ski in Austria. At age 3, I was fiercely independent and one morning in Austria I took myself off and caught a bus to the ski slopes.

I was fearless and navigating the ski bus whilst carrying my skies. Caught two chair lifts and arrived at my destination, the top of the mountain.

Thankfully, a Ski Instructor saw this little red skier taking off like a bullet and hurtling towards the cliff edge. He scooped me up before I disappeared off the edge. Hours later I was finally re-united with my very distressed family. In Austria I would come home from Kindergarten ski-school speaking German, adapting and learning new skills fast.

Whilst holidaying in France, we were riding bicycles on an island. At 5 years old I chose a different path to everyone else, and ended up hurtling down a narrow, bumpy track on the cliff edge. My family took the path above the coastal cliff, the safe path. Our Mum later recalled that she was screaming, "keep peddling!" at the top of her lungs. Her heart in her mouth because as I reached the halfway point, I started to slow down as if I was going to stop. I needed to pee, and the screaming got louder, "keep going!" As I reached the safety zone, I was re-united with my family and had that needed pee. Being held tight by my parents, emotionally relieved that I was safe. In France my sister and I would often collect the breakfast from the bakery, speaking only in French. Our parents gave us great opportunities to take responsibility, build independence and to explore different cultures. In reflection, to walk a free-spirited path was evident, and part of my true nature. Our mum really had her hands full, as I was non-stop and fiercely independent. Our childhood was fabulous, and we never went without love; Mum was amazing, and we did all the activities we loved, as an active, outdoors family, creative expression was encouraged and supported.

Our Dad was doing and being the best, he knew, and this goes for all parents. We can only do, be and give from what we know and think we know at the time. There is no such thing as perfection, and as a parent if you think it is about being perfect, then let me ask you this? How will your children ever match up when you are always right? They may start to feel inadequate and form a limiting belief of, *'I am not good enough'*.

From an early age I would use my favourite teddy bear for those nice feelings of pleasure. I recall masturbating and being busted by my mum at nine years old while doing my homework and I started to feel some shame inside – like I was doing something wrong. I was never made to feel this, and it was a normal interpretation of being caught. I am sure we have all been busted in the act!

We took an eight-week holiday of a lifetime to Canada and America after our parents separated. While in America my sister and I did a funny show where we dressed up as old ladies, the Edna and Grace show, it was hilarious, and our imaginations were grand. We went on an awesome fishing trip in California, where my sister caught the biggest catch of the day and I was found downstairs, watching and learning how to play poker with the men.

I have so many great memories, like going to a shopping centre late at night and having the best and biggest pizza ever. Going to Disneyland, panning for gold at Knott's Berry farm and talking to a Robot for hours asking very funny questions was a trip of a lifetime. We travelled through central America on the Greyhound buses, hiked in the Rocky Mountains and went swimming in cool glacial flow-off in the river creeks. It was the best holiday ever.

In America I proposed to a friend of the family, "Will you marry my mommy too?" I really wanted a Daddy and the perfect family, and I thought anything was possible in America. They thought it was beautiful and such a normal response for a six-year-old.

I was found in many of the photos curled up in his lap. The cuddles soothed the loss of my dad and being held by the masculine, I felt safe. I was hurting, lost and one of the best decisions our Mum made. We restored our unstable family to safe foundations, a stable family of three.

Like many young girls in the 1970's, we loved to dress up in our parents' sexy lingerie, and we would often dress in my friends' mums' underwear, stockings, and heels. I have boys, so am unsure if girls still do this. It was very natural and all innocent play. I loved to play and wear sexy lingerie, it was fun.

When we moved to Wales at eight years old, I tasted power games. I was different from other girls and good at sport. Also, our mum was the only single parent in the small village and people wanted to know one another's business, in a loving and yet very nosy way. This was made even worse when I invented an imaginary older brother who was away in the army. That would have made my mum a teenage mother with him, which was untrue, still they gossiped. Deep down I longed for the male presence and a brother for protection. It was girls pushing boundaries and seeing how far they could push before I snapped.

Time is a great healer; it was a game of testing boundaries with one another and only lasted a short while. We had ponies in a local field and mum really made it the best opportunity for us.

We wore hand me down fashion, as it is what became our normal and the latest sneakers were never an issue. We were regularly active in gymnastics, canoeing, horses and athletics. I guess that is why I now love shopping in the markets.

Going off on backpack adventures with friends on our pony's was very normal, it was never dull, and I have been told I was fun to be around. We played with Ouija boards and totally freaked ourselves out.

We made dens, we made up 'clubs', and would go skating in Wellington boots across the mud flats of the Cleddau river. It was sinking mud and we would often come home with our dogs smelling of Canada geese poo.

We would get a ride to gymnastics on the back of one of our friend's dad's milk float, it was awesome, totally open and we thought we were super cool. It was the best fun ever, having slush puppies at the end of a long gymnastic training session and life was freer in Wales, it was a time-warp, 30 years behind anywhere else.

At 10 ½ years old I had my first bleed and entered the Goddess phase. This was a massive celebration in our home, my mum and sister getting out a variety of panty-liners, so I could learn what to do. It was party celebration time, my chest was flat, and I was obsessed with breasts, doing anything I could to make them grow, pulling them and listening to my sister who told me to eat Polo mints (they are the mint with the hole in) and if I ate them then they would grow- funny! They stayed an A cup. I got my first bra, a size 28AA, yes as flat as a pancake when I was 10 years old. I was blessed with a butt and no boobs. I was so happy to be going to junior school with a bra on, I felt so cool and would lean forward in class, so the boys could see my bra straps through a white t-shirt. I thought I was so cool and grown-up. In Wales, no one cared about fashion, we were too busy having adventures, getting up to mischief and pushing the edges of life. We were curious and seeking beyond what we were being told. I loved secondary school, and I recall being a handful. Cheeky, fearless and challenging authority.

They were such fun years, and many stories that I look forward to laughing about when I take my family back to visit this special place in Pembrokeshire. A piece of my heart still calls home, and yet home is within. Mum followed her heart by moving our family to Wales.

In my dressage lesson at 11 years old, I was told to soften my hips more and make love to the saddle. I replied, "I have never had sex', the response was *"imagine"*, so I did. It made me horny that a few times while out riding my pony, I rubbed myself to orgasm on the pommel of the saddle, and then later while out fox hunting at fifteen years.

Around 12-13 years old, I began exploring with boys, where I began healthy sensual exploration with girls from the age of 9-11 years old. Almost but not quite was a theme, much touching and exploring sensations in the woods.

A few years later during Pony Club camp, with raging hormones, I was busted after an adventure of innocent sensual exploration of teenage play.

The next day after the caravan adventures I was representing the pony club, show jumping in a big event. The baby of the team and we qualified for the National Show jumping Championships. The funny part was that my pony was called *'Bimbo'*. Little did I know what a Bimbo was at eleven years old, and wow could that Pony jump and had a huge heart of courage. He was only fourteen hands, wore his heart on his sleeve, gave it 111%, was courageous and a free spirit. A perfect teacher and reflection of his young rider, both courageously learning and growing with one another.

At twelve years old, I was playing native Indians on horseback, when I had a riding accident. It was a moment when you are called by your parent and you ignore it with an "in a minute reply". I carried on playing, vaulting over my pony with ease while he was galloping and ended up slipping in horse poo. As he galloped off, I looked up, and was accidentally being kicked in the mouth. 'In a minute' became me losing three of my main second top teeth. I was lucky as an inch higher or lower and I would not be here to share my story.

Losing my teeth was nothing new. I lost baby teeth whilst jumping in the swimming pool as a toddler. My mum recalls being told at the time by the dentist that the tooth if found can be pushed back in. So back to the horse show field with torches in hand, on a mission to find missing teeth. One top main tooth and incisor was found and pushed back in by the dentist. This was an attempt to allow the root nerves to re-take. He advised me to take up swimming, so we increased my swimming training and at the end of a session whilst messing around I duck-dived and cracked the same teeth on the bottom of the pool. The cement cracked, and it would be years later that I chose to get a bridge as the tooth never took and I was needing new teeth. Then another ten years later I went down a long 2 ½ year path of reconstructive cosmetic dentistry with teeth implants. I am blessed to now have sexy teeth, in my 40's.

I had another head trauma on the same pony at the age of thirteen while competing in a cross-country event. I went to jump a solid fence, he stopped, and I carried on through the air, my head splitting the telegraph pole. Yes, part of the solid jump, in half with my head. Luckily, I was wearing a crash helmet and spinal support; I got off lightly with a head concussion.

At twelve I had a skiing accident where I tore my left knee cartilage and ruptured my ACL (anterior cruciate ligament) while on a skiing holiday with Dad.

Adventurous Encounters

As teenagers we were inquisitive and curious

Learning about one another

Testing the boundaries

Daring one another

Hormones were raging

Anticipation waiting

Our known reality

Finding our place in society

Childhood into adolescents

Testing the limits

Exploratory and fun

Valuable lessons between girls and boys

Our innocence explored

For many remaining intact

Exploring with one another

In the safety with friends

Warm fuzzy feelings

Puberty hormones awakening

LIFE'S BLUEPRINT

We played games like squeak, piggy squeak

Playing with innocence

Blindfolded one by one

Sitting on one another's knees

Daring for some

Guessing whose knee, you were sitting upon

Playful innocence, Touching, exploring

Simple fun!

Especially as there were boys in the room

Secret crushes and hormonal rushes

Feeling more daring as the night went on

Progressing to kissing

Exploring with one another

Feeling their energy

Pony club camping

Breaking boy's voices, becoming men

From removing items of clothes

To spinning the bottle

We became more daring

In a group with one another

Testing the boundaries

Egging one another on

The excitement of being caught

Added to the fun

A fear of being caught

All very innocent and

Oh, so beautiful exploration

The Goddess/Maiden

A natural transition

Sacred journey into womanhood

The night got leaked out

We each got to own it

To respond to the rumour

Our innocent worlds fell apart

Embarrassed and humiliated

Called a slut behind my back

The boys a slap on the back

Cut like a knife!

LIFE'S BLUEPRINT

Natural self-exploration

Tainted with shame and hate

It was all simple innocent and playful fun

Shame and guilt left within

Many blaming, the others avoiding

To step up and own it

Even though it cut deep within

A knowing deep feeling of

Never wanting to be called that slut again!

Time passed, and the rumours settled

Making way for new beginnings

Our spirits free and pushing the limits

Our inner wild never to be tamed again

Yet deep within carrying some blame

Guilt wrestling, strangling within

Sexually exploratory, suppressed expression

Building anger and mounting suppression deviance awakened

These toxic emotions stinking of shit

Carries you around until ready to shift

Self-responsibility and owning your stuff
Forgiving all, embracing loving thoughts
To develop self-respect and dissolve hate within.
To honour and own your inner slut!

On my pony jumping hurdles (top), and with my sister (below)

In 2011, I came across the brilliant work of Louise L. Hay and her great book 'You Can Heal Your Life'. Within, she paints a picture of how illnesses and accidents manifest as a direct reflection of our inner world (thoughts, emotions and beliefs), as well as metaphysical meaning of various body areas. There may be other factors at play to create symptoms. These 'symptoms' as they are perceived resonate with My soul truth. The more you wake-up from the deep sleep, the clearer you begin to see the raw uncut truth. Throughout this book, and as you read my life experiences and the biological or psychological conditions, the following glossary is of those and their metaphysical meaning. Perhaps you can relate so some of these too!?

Accidents: Inability to speak up for the self

Amenorrhea: Not wanting to be a woman and a dislike of self.

Addictions: Running from the self, fear, not knowing how to love the self

Anorexia: Denying the self-life, extreme fear, self-hatred and rejection- a way to control.

Anxiety: Not trusting the flow and process of life.

Arthritis: Feeling unloved, criticism and resentment.

Bed-wetting: Fear of a parent, usually the father. I was a bed wetter until I was 12 years old. It ended by having a machine on my bed that would become activated with liquid.

Bulimia: Hopeless terror, frantic stuffing and purging of self-hatred.

Cancer: Deep hurt and long-standing resentment, carrying hatreds.

Candida: Feeling very scattered, frustration and anger. Demanding, lack of trust in relationships and great takers.

Depression: Anger you do not feel you have a right to have and hopelessness

Dysmenorrhea: Anger at the self, hatred of the body and of being a woman.

Epstein-Barr Virus: Pushing beyond one's limits, fear of not being good enough, draining all inner support, and stress. Frigidity: Fear, denial of pleasure, a belief that sex is bad, fear of father

Genital warts – Human Papilloma Virus: Little expressions of hate and belief in your ugliness.

Herpes Genitalis: Mass belief in sexual guilt and need for punishment, public shame and a belief of punishment from God and rejection of the genitals.

Knees: A bridge between the spiritual and physical dimensions. Knees also represent pride and ego, stubborn ego and pride – an inability to bend – inflexibility. I will often work much on the knees, as they tell a story.

Tonsillitis: Fear, repressed emotions, stifled creativity. Thrush: Anger over making the wrong decisions.

Urinary tract infections: Pissed off, usually with the opposite sex. Blaming others. I also have a duplex kidney, of which 9% of the population also has, so three kidneys!

At twelve I found my first pornographic magazine and what I saw was different to mine. My labia were more swollen, and my inner labia protruded. I am not sure if image photo-shop was around then, but the vaginas were neat and tidy. I enjoyed looking at women and was becoming naturally curious in my sensuality. Looking at women, I also began to be aroused and more curious.

I started to become self-conscious and obsessed, checking myself out every time I went to the bathroom and became self-conscious in the school showers. I recall a PE (Physical Education) teacher who would pull our towels off us, so we had to all shower together. This was humiliating for any teenage girl who started to want her privacy.

There was a shame in our bodies and not the freedom I now have. We would rather stay dirty all day after sport than have a shower.

I desperately wanted a neat and tidy Vagina, that over the years I almost broke a few toilet seats standing on them to take a closer look!

There is nothing worse than being made to shower when you have your period and are wearing a pad, for any teenager you desire privacy, your voice to be heard and not feel humiliated.

This has empowered me to embrace my sexy and voluptuous pink bits. We are given our unique bodies, to grow into and love. Take a deep breath, this may shock some!

A couple of times at the tender age of twelve years old I found myself in the bathroom with the door locked and thinking about slicing bits off.

Okay, breathe.

Rewind to a very shocking time where I was crying my heart out and screaming on the inside, a cold razor blade in one hand and my inner labia in the other. Ready to nip and tuck! I had developed a deep self-loathing and hate for the way I looked down there and even my face.

I would compare myself to my sister, who is beautiful, yet I was unable to see my own beauty. I had to learn to grow into my own skin, all part of my journey back to the empowered self. Yes, the thought is horrific, right?

I felt ugly, deep rage within and was angry at the world. Why me?

Many thoughts of shame, blame, guilt and self-disgust running through my mind.

Why am I so different? I want to be normal.

Wow, how many times have others done this; females with your vagina/pussy/yoni, or maybe men with your penis/dick/lingam, or any other beautiful body part that you are finding challenging to accept as you?

How many times do we compare ourselves to our friends, be it their shape, size or looks?

Thankfully, I left my bits intact and its full glory and voluptuous beauty. This is a huge topic and one that is explored within *Wildflower – Remembering a Sacred Place*. This is for both men and women learning how to honour the yoni as a sacred place. This limiting belief went on to create issues with urine infections, sexually transmitted diseases, viruses and growing up had a few pap smears come back as precancerous CIN1 and one CIN3. I was also having thrush every week while in my early 20's.

Even though I was struggling with body dysmorphia on the inside, I had zero challenge with going skinny dipping at 15 and 16 years old (maybe it was the alcohol we were sneaking). I recall sneaking out of the club to go skinny dipping with friends to then get dressed and return to the club looking like a drowned rat. Funny stories of skinny dipping in Ibiza with my sister and losing my knickers.

Can you imagine the horror of a 14-year-old walking onto the crowded beach to see her knickers next to a couple sunbaking? Yes, life was fun and pushing the edges was very normal. Life was never dull.

The healthier a body becomes, then the virus can no longer remain there, and in my early 30's eliminated the HPV from my body. Anyone can do this. Now they give vaccines to teenagers. Yet, the underlying cause remains! I do not really advocate the vaccines, as the cause will express in another way.

We refused in 2019 for our son to have the HPV vaccine, even if they are potential carriers. What was interesting was the venomous response and attack from others for our making this very personal choice as a family. One person even said, *"if my daughter gets cancer it is because of your son's dirty prick."* I find humans in-human and plain ignorant when fear gets in the way. Fear is more likely to cause cancer than anything else.

My distorted body image started young, teased about the way I looked, my ears stuck out and had buck teeth. I landed the names Dumbo and Goofy.

At 12-years old I had my ears pinned back, as I felt rejected, ugly and teased for the way I looked. Girls were mean about the way you looked, and I wished to feel good when I tucked my hair behind my ears or when I put it up. It was one of the best things I had done, and all on the National Health Service.

My eldest son reminded me of the phrase *'Sticks and stones may hurt your bones, but names will never hurt you'*, and agrees is absolute bullshit when you are a kid. I found myself saying it to him and he said, "words hurt."

Yes true, names do hurt and cut, and they also carry a harmful and toxic vibration. They stick like dog shit on your shoe, and over time we must learn and become more resilient by creating a gentle yet powerful armour of confidence, so they no longer bring harm. It is time to stop and block the harmful taunts from others and to those who speak mean words, say *'Thank you and Fu3k you'*, and hand it back to them with a smile. You get to choose!

Girls can be mean bitches, hence why I had a strong resonance with men until I fully embraced the woman that I am today. Women can be mean, and so too can men get the bitch in them, and it is time to stop. Women get high-jacked by comparison and many are so stuck in fear and shame that a woman who knows herself is seen as a threat. It is time to love our fellow sisters and brothers and become one soul family. I am grateful for the strong and fierce women in my life. Everyone be nice!

Some teenagers are afraid to approach their parents' and nowadays the Internet has pretty much everything available at the press of a button, with a lot more on offer too! It is so vital to always be open and available with a non-judgemental attitude for children as they grow into teenagers.

"Women supporting one another and passing on wisdom."

It is vital for wise women to get together, protecting and guiding the younger women through these early stages with tender loving care. I tasted bullying in secondary school from girls in the other school and had a few gangs, gang up on me, I learnt how to fight back, take on more than one at a time and survive! It was all based from jealousy of boys I was kissing, being different and excelling at sport. I was living with anger, fear of abandonment and I had self-loathing of my body.

School was fun and we would often kiss one another at lunch time behind the Welsh room. Great memories and lip, tongue repertoire.

A Perfect Lesson

At sixteen going on seventeen years old, we moved from Wales to England and I started a new high school. I got on well with the boys and the girls did not like me. I was good at hockey and this put a few noses out of joint. I started to miss school and instead would go to where my horse was stabled. My mum found out. I said I felt sick with a sore throat and I was also getting tired. I did not want to say anything about the nasty taunts and bullying from the girls. The doctor did a blood test and confirmed glandular fever (Epstein-Barr virus). I left the school and had some time out. I spent the next 3 months mostly in bed sleeping and going to see my horse, which was healing on many levels, he understood my emotions and we trusted one another.

> *"I chose to come back and experience adversity, so I could heal from the inside out, to guide others. It also took me a long time to wake-up from sleeping. The path of soul remembrance."*
>
> – Zoe Anna

I left the school, taking a year out. In the New Year, I ended up getting the left anterior cruciate ligament (ACL) in my knee repaired. I had torn it slightly on the skiing accident, then while exercising an event horse I managed to fully tear it. I went to see an Orthopaedic surgeon in Oxford, England, who was Australian and trained with the greats of Merve Cross.

He was the Orthopaedic wizard of knees here in Sydney in the 1980's and 90's. He reconstructed my knee using some of my quadriceps muscle.

During the recovery of my knee repair, my dad offered to join them on an overseas holiday with my step-mum; a great place to rest. As soon as we arrived in Menorca, my dad and I were arguing about something stupid, and we had a car crash.

He said it was my fault we crashed, and I felt anger and inner rage. Before we had the crash, we were both arguing, and I was being a proverbial pain in the ass. I was angry and pushing to feel loved.

While on this holiday with my dad and step-mum I had a very intense argument with him. I stormed off on crutches, got drunk with some locals, got in their car, went to a club on the opposite side of the island, then returned to the hotel late that night. Little did I know I was followed back by one of them. The hours that followed would be the most horrific and violent six hours of my life. I was raped over and over. I went into survival mode and prayed silently through salty tears that he would leave when he was finished. I kept quiet in fear of him hurting me even more than he had already. With the fear please do not let me get pregnant. I was unable to run, unable to scream and was locked in the room.

I was immobilised by fear and then the emotional numbness set in. Feelings of worthlessness, helplessness and hopelessness. The next morning, the hotel asked for my passport and extra money for my guest! Or they would keep my passport.

I paid money to get raped.

I felt dirty, cheap and shameful.

I was filled with rage, feeling trapped.

I was silent with this secret for two years.

Those silent years, I pushed it down and this is when the bulimia began. I was numb and pushed my emotions deep down. It was during a game of truth or dare at Boarding school, that it all came out. Imagine taking the top off a pressure cooker, or when the top of a volcano blows and that will give you an insight into what was going on inside my body, mind and soul. After telling friends, I flipped out and set off the fire alarm for the girls boarding house.

That was the first time I had told anyone, and it would result in my first out of body experience. I am sure this was a way to separate my spiritual from the physical as the emotions were overwhelming. It was like being kicked out of my body for my own sanity, and to ensure my nervous system did not blow and short circuit; shock can do this.

I was floating above my body and watching the whole scene, it was weird and surreal. I was in shock and the intensity of the emotions separated my spiritual 'astral body' from my physical body. I saw the entire Boarding house out on the lawn, late at night whilst watching myself screaming and crying. I felt a jolt, like a pulling on the umbilical cord and I came back down into my body, it was like being sucked in through my crown energy centre and down into my body, like a body bag zipping me back in.

I began rape counselling and had my family support. I was prescribed Valium by my GP, and if a class got too much, I was excused, and the House Mistress would give me a Valium. I slept much and this is when the self-harm began. I would bang my head against the wall and punch the wall until I felt something beyond the numbness.

Later, I was suspended for breaking out of school one night with my girlfriend. They termed it vandalism as what we created looked like a religious ritual; we were playing and allowing our creativity to be expressed. I was angry, hurting and screaming silently on the inside and started to use sex to feel loved and wanted. I was searching for moments of intimate connection to feel something.

The emptiness and loneliness grew darker inside and the crying out to be loved grew louder. Unconsciously, I became a master of manipulation, games and this was the beginning of the victim programming.

I learned to be a people-pleaser, rebelled at authority and when it came to relationships, I rejected my inner No, I did not know how to love myself. It was easier to reject my inner desires, as to be rejected by others felt like death itself. It would be in our dad's final weeks of life, that I began to truly open to love and forgive our Dad. As we sat across from one another, sharing from our raw hearts, we both realised we were very much alike one another. The child that had been pushed away, neglected and her no rejected, began a soul's journey to begin receiving love. Once I forgave and fully embraced the imperfections of my dad with forgiveness then all future relationships with men began to shift. I had to re-learn how to have a relationship with self, my inner-child and open the door to my vulnerable heart.

I had recurring bouts of tonsillitis more frequently, so they had to be removed. Following the tonsillectomy, the obsession with food began. I started to control my eating, by not eating. I was diagnosed with Anorexia Nervosa, which rapidly was accompanied with Bulimia. I felt out of control and eating was something I began to use to gain control. The rape, suppressing my voice, and screaming out on the inside needed an outlet. I was pushing down the emotions with my fingers, numbing out. It was not enough, and my choices escalated into alcohol, drugs, self-harm and unconscious sex.

Self-harm was punching a concrete wall with my bare fists until they bled and punching myself in the head. I felt no pain as I had become so numb. I developed depression, had moments of suicidal ideation and the bulimia continued into my mid-thirties. It finally stopped when I became responsible for another life, a magical pregnancy with our first son.

In my thirties I was re-diagnosed with anxiety, depression and PTSD (post-traumatic stress disorder), which had an impact upon low desire for my sexual exploration. I was stuck inside my mind, which was distorted with the emotions of worthlessness, hopelessness and helplessness, and I was living and functioning in survival mode.

In relationships, I had anxiety and fear of them leaving me, and lived a life of constant disappointment. I was addicted to playing the victim, addicted to partying at the weekends and addicted to pushing my body to its max to numb out. I was stuck in my head and many times living in a place of fantasy as my reality felt like insanity at times. Fantasy can be a great survival tool to get you through the reality.

This will be hard for my beautiful family to see, though with much love and compassion, this is only my humble opinion, to be where I stand now. I became unconsciously trapped within the cycle of the victim and the rescuer. As a parent I now understand, and this is challenging and heartbreaking to hear for any parent or sibling to witness the person they love in self-destruct mode, so be the observer, picking up the pieces along the way. This is the journey of life, we each have to find our own unique path through it all and there is no right or wrong and no blame either, it is what it is. Every parent wishes to protect their child.

The games we play become entangled upon and within our subconscious; we are all learning and growing, and it is all about personal responsibility and I am blessed for the colourful journey!

Love is expanding, as is a painful path, the bitter sweetness of love.

Having said all this, I loved school and all the friendships I experienced. I was busy every lunch time with gymnastics training, orchestra practice, swimming squad and hockey practice. I represented the County/State in swimming, gymnastics, athletics, cross-country running and was experienced in horsemanship.

Competing in the National Tetrathlon Championships I was shortlisted for the Welsh team. Tetrathlon, is four events, including swimming, pistol shooting, a cross-country event on your horse and cross-country running, held over two days. My pony became lame and I missed out representing Wales in the Nationals.

I used to compete in affiliated show jumping and competed in one day horse events and many Horse shows at the weekend. Even at the age of 10 years we would go out for all-day adventures with a picnic and our ponies in the Welsh countryside, we had so much fun. I was a talented cellist, acquiring Grade VII at the age of 15 years, and had a fantastic life with my mum and sister. Wales was home, no one cared what you wore, and the outdoors was our playground. It has been challenging to put these events into order.

LIFE'S BLUEPRINT

Abandonment

I was stuck in the game of abandonment
An inner vice, a slow demise
Tainted with sorrow and wrestling
With disappointment
The only freedom lay deep within.

My inner world perception
Became my projection
Manipulating my soul
Misconception and
Deception of truth.
Anger at the world
A toxic suppression,
Choking my sacred spirit
Attracting the perfect teachers.

Invited unconsciously
And a fucker makes my day attitude
Like a bull terrier with a bone
I gave as well as I got
Never backing down.

BREAKING FREE

I would fight till the end
And never stay down
The need to be right.
My inner wild exploding
Imploding into self-destruct
Eventually out cold
Silenced within.

Fighting with a man
I came off the worst
Smashed up face
Broken noses
Blood splattered clothes
Hurting heart in tatters

In the dark of the night
Back in their arms
Desperate for love
A moment of sweet delight
An anti-dote to the pain
Feeding off one another

LIFE'S BLUEPRINT

Like starved parasites
Sucking one another's souls dry.
Abusive relationship
One by one
Sexual, emotional, psychological
It's all the same
Dis-empowered and hopeless within
Stuck in the prison
Self-created prism of pain
Numb on the inside
Lost within.

My inner voice suppressed
My cries unheard
Daily self-punishment
Of self-loathing and hate
It all came back to me
The perfect teachers
To honour my soul
And love my spirit.

To move past fear and

Welcome in courage

To move forward

And Stop

Disrespecting my truth.

The journey back to self-love

Self-worth of being

To let go of the struggle of fixer and pleaser

Embrace the beautiful soul within

Never to dis-honour

My spirit again!

There was all this stuck energy, and I had no idea how to control it, work with it or release it. I experienced abdominal pain, painful periods and abdominal bloating. Diagnosed with IBS (irritable bowel syndrome) I went onto medication; it would be years later during my Yoga journey that I realised these issues were due to a combination of shallow breathing and internal worry. I am also gut sensitive, so in times of stress my gut is affected. The gut and sacral area is where I get my intuitive messages; it is a great and wise receptacle.

At eighteen years old, I had my first serious boyfriend with whom I fell in love, he was a few years younger at just 16. I was emotionally still sixteen years old, and I chose to lose my virginity again, my way, in full ownership. It was a magical and beautiful experience.

The sixteen-year journey with bulimia was a way to feel a release from the internal pain and deep-rooted anger. I was addicted to hurting myself, which made me feel good, I felt worthless, hopeless and was pushing away self-love. I found a way to have a 'let-down' of the anger and frustration.

I desperately wanted to feel loved and was running again!

My options were running out as I had burnt many bridges. I did not mean to use people. I was disconnected from who I was and caught within a paradigm of survival mode of running nowhere! Stuck in the merry-go around of hopelessness and self-destruction.

After leaving Boarding school I went to a Crammer (sixth form) college at 19 years old to re-sit my exams. I met some interesting and beautiful people. On my way to see a friend before college, I received a distressed and sickening phone call. She was found lying outside on the concrete beneath her bedroom window, dead. This changed me forever. I feel her spirit with me, dancing within my heart and reminding me to live life to the full.

She was a beautiful soul, full of life and vibrancy, and is part of who I am today! I lost a dear friend and learned to let go even more, gaining a deeper insight into the tragedy of death for a soul gone too young. She was off on another new soul adventure.

Later that year, I started working with horses in England and Europe as a groom. I was passionate about horses and talented in horsemanship. I knew that I wanted to do something I was passionate about, and I had no idea what?

I felt like a fuck-up and seemed to attract more of the unwanted into my life. Looking back, I can see that now. I was a manifesto magnet.

I worked in Europe on a stud farm, and I loved the hard work. We were up at 4.30 am and would muck out fifteen horses, sweep the yard, exercise horses, and learn the science and complexity of artificial insemination; Stallion semen was expensive!

I would take the frisky fillies out in the ménage, to be shown. I enjoyed the challenge and had a natural ease and intuitive way with horses. After a few weeks there were advances made towards me. It takes two to tango and I would have been flirting and hungry for attention on the inside, he was older and cute. He was my boss.

The conditions that we were working within were tough, and a few times we were told to get back out in the yard at night in our pyjamas to sweep the whole yard again. If there was one piece of straw left, then this would become a bigger pile of straw. Looking back, we were being broken-in, learning about hard work, discipline and taking pride in the area we worked in. We would drop into bed exhausted at the end of the day and then up again for a 0430hr start. We often were not allowed to wear our crash hats and one of the girls got crushed under a stallion. I was the untamed wild filly, hence why I connected well with them. They would follow my guide as their lead, and they would dance and prance around.

It was magical as our free-spirited energies connected.

It was beautiful to observe as I had a gift with horses and the horse spirit. Safety was not high on the list and the final straw came by getting uncomfortable with always having to walk through my bosses' bedroom to get to my own bed and feeling the energy of a move on me. I was packed and out of there, running again.

I was a wild filly with a strong spirit!

While finding my way through life, I was constantly reliving my story, wearing my heart on my sleeve as an open book. There are many years a blur still to this day, and have no relevance, except to give You the reader an insight into some of the adventures and lessons whilst growing. I went from one frying pan into another, from Belgium to arriving at a Polo yard as one of the horse grooms. I loved the work as a groom, it was fun, physically hard and this assisted with refocusing my mind and working off the surplus of energy. Hanging out with horses all day was heaven, taking out three ponies at the same time and feeling I was living the dream.

During my short stay here, there was a massive argument with one of the grooms. I had a big mouth, had no care how I used it, fearlessly standing up to others that were being bossy. I never thought far enough ahead to the bigger picture and consequences. I was lost and screaming out to be loved and in all the wrong places. My boss was beautiful and saw what I was yet to discover fundamentals to honouring my safety and boundaries. He saw my *wild spirited and wounded soul*. He was also aware of what was about to take place at the polo yard.

One day we had the sad news of half of the ponies being taken away for slaughtering. I recall throwing my arms around their necks and balling my eyes out. A final long embrace before they were taken away. It still chokes me. Now with fewer ponies they had to let a groom go, he was kind and offered me a full month of pay. He was protecting me from the bigger picture. He knew how feisty and wild I was, and no doubt would have seen my traumatic past, in my body language and eyes.

He was a master of understanding the behaviour of horses and I connected on a deep spirit level with them. I would have kicked and bolted like a horse until I was beaten and broken, my spirit suppressed. You see, when the Argentinian players came over, it would also be my role as a female groom, to be available whenever and wherever they chose to have me, yes, be available for sex and their fun! I am grateful, he opened the doorway for me to choose to step away.

My favourite book at the time, that I read over and over was Riders by Jacqui Collins. Jake Lovell the Gypsy had dark curly hair, dark eyes and a beautiful wild and untamed spirit. I had a massive crush on him, he was my favourite character. Rupert was my least favourite as he would overpower women, treat them like pigs and take what he wanted, without asking! There were lots of raunchy sex scenes, partner swapping, moments of romance, show jumping and a love for horses. I got to explore my fantasies with my mind.

Many teenagers or young adults must decide what job you want to do? It's a crazy thought, when most of your beliefs are based upon those of your parents or caregivers, and honestly much of it didn't make sense to me. It was a start to get me out of the rut I was in after the short-lived career as a groom.

My early twenties were a drug hazed blur, I had fun yet can remember little. I graduated with a High National Diploma in Nursing at twenty-three years and hopped from one abusive relationship to another. I attracted partners that I would end up hurting and pushing away, to replace them with ones that would put me down and treat me disrespectfully in front of others. I was a fighter and it also gave me the will to survive, to walk alone and never stop giving up for what I believed in. Having to lie after my face got messed up became easier, as deep down I felt I deserved it. I felt not worthy and I believed he loved me. We needed one another and we fed off each other like a toxic virus.

Welcome to the *co-dependent toxic relationship*. This was physically, emotionally, psychologically abusive. We also attracted one another, and as hard as it may be for some to recognise, we were there to learn from contrast from one another. When you are in it, you are blind!

During my Nurse practical placement (internship), I was removed from where I was to complete my training, after I disclosed the abuse and facets of what I had experienced. 'They' claimed I was a threat to patients and suspended as, 'unsafe to practice'. I felt my trust had been broken. Thankfully, my dad, a GP contacted the doctor who did my mental health assessment, and he gave my dad a message, "Tell your daughter to not talk about her story, when she comes to her final assessment". He also gave my mum a message, "Zoe needs to work with youth when she is older, as she understands what it is like to not be understood and she really gets them." A proud moment to have found my way out of the rough of life and realising here was a deeper reason for experiencing all that I did and why this series has been modified to accommodate youth.

Back to the story.

The final psychiatric assessment went smoothly, and I was relocated to another hospital to finish my Nursing internship. I learnt to adapt to different documentation, a new area of specialty, and the bar of challenge was raised. I am grateful as I grew in many ways, embraced the challenges, overcame adversity, stepped up to the plate, and expressed my truth. Here is a recollection of the experience through verse. Even when the odds were against me, the fighter inside rose and stood her ground. I was honouring my self-worth and fighting for my voice to be heard!

Step up

In life we meet resistance
To accelerate our growth
To step up and be free
Or be pushed back into adversity

The bar was raised to pass the test
A new hospital to prove my worth
Under the pump to be the change
To honour my greatness and shine within

The stakes were against me
My reputation under the microscope
Every move, under the watchful eyes
Not one, but five assessors
I rose to the challenge
Courageous and fearless
I would overcome and achieve this mission.

Not taking No for an answer
To finding a solution with ease

LIFE'S BLUEPRINT

Proving my ability as a great Nurse

Standing proud in my accomplishment

A passion to help others

Awakened a desire within my heart

Standing proud in my truth

I found my voice and expressed my worth

No longer a doormat I expressed from my heart

Nothing was going to stop me

I had so much to share and

It was now or never

Here are the words that came out that day

Raw and authentic, in every way

'You are very small people in my big wide world,

That I am yet to discover

You try to block me and get in my way

I will mow you all down,

I am here for great things

As my spirit will never be suppressed again.'

They passed me
Following a tough interrogation
Attempts to bring me down
Now brushed aside
They saw the passion and depth of the
Young woman who had changed
Risen and grown inside.
From taking back her power
Of self-responsibility
Free from the victim
Ownership of her actions
No longer hiding within.

Looking back, the bold words I expressed at the time were powerful to myself. I completed my professional Nursing training and my family came to celebrate with me at my graduation. I was hurting on the inside, and it was after the graduation presentation, that I broke down in tears and told them the truth. They had passed me yet refused to sign my document of good character, which meant you could not get a job! My family was supportive, rightfully angry, and we celebrated the fact that I was a great person. We would find a way.

It was three months later that I began work, 'undercover', at a Nursing home. A beautiful soul, that believed in me and became a major influence in my nursing career and life.

A psychiatric nurse, who saw the diamond within, and she created the perfect way so I could be free. For three months I was known by the name, 'Rachael'. One of the assistant nurses was the son of one of the heads of the college. It was then that I found out that there had been a major breech in confidentiality, and leaking of information where raw, intimate and private details of my traumas had been shared over the family dinner table. It was a time to stay silent, and to see that I was being guided by a soul who saw the greatness that I was unable to see at the time. I am eternally grateful. In life, it is vital to have a select few people that really believe in us and make choices beyond the box of limitations.

Rewinding back, this brings tears to my eyes at the way souls can be so inhumane and ignorant. From working under-cover, I was able to get a job, and I began to realise the power of silence. The next job would bring me closer to my dad and an opportunity to work near him. A special time to re-kindle a relationship, and it was also one of the first hospitals he had worked in.

The day before I was about to leave, they called to say they could not employ me, due to my record of bad character. I felt heartbroken, rejected, abandoned and hit rock bottom. I flipped and went off the rails.

It would be a year later that I returned to Nursing, after Mum came and got me out me out of a drug haze of partying in fields, lost and exploring ways to find myself. The sacred times in life are when you drop all your reasons for what you think you know and be nourished by those that love you.

I left Somerset and moved back in with my mum and stepdad for some tender loving care. I had not been looking after myself, living with self-neglect and denial. Whilst applying for jobs I had much inner resistance; I recall hearing about Princess Diana being tragically killed in a car crash in Paris. It was as clear as day and reminded me to wake up and do something meaningful with my life.

During my Nurse training, I took up a position as a night care assistant for an ex-Royal Marine. A special soul I wish to write about, had paralysis of all four limbs following an accident where his spinal cord was damaged. He had a major impact on my life, in the way I see things, and to be eternally grateful - no matter what life delivers.

He had just got back from Iraq and felt a massive need to sleep with as many women as possible. It was almost like his subconscious knew something for he wanted to sleep with everything in sight. His mates had a big night out planned and he was looking for a quiet night; this was unusual for him. After much persuasion he went out and ignored his intuition. He got drunk, and later that night jumped headfirst into a water fountain. He knew as soon as he hit the bottom, his neck was broken. His life dramatically changed. When we met, his mates had raised enough money, so he could live in a self-contained house.

As his experience living in a Nursing home at twenty-four years old was disturbing. We talked about everything and nothing, the time before his accident, what he would do when research made it so he could walk again, and even re-design our new nursing outfits into Baywatch swimsuits. We talked about sex and death, and how we were each other's female and male doubles, even with our looks, and many times the dreams he had about walking, running, and fucking the first woman in sight. He was always walking in his dreams; never did he see himself in a wheelchair.

As part of his therapeutic care, I had to roll him joints, as the marijuana was great for his spasms. We got so stoned once, we had run out of some equipment and I had to call the Community Nurse. We laughed so much as it was a time when you are meant to keep your shit together, yet laughter takes over. This Nurse was super cool, and a beautiful soul with whom I had encountered on practical placement assessments. We felt invincible, wild and finding as much freedom as we could in his world that had physical limitations.

I completed my time working there, and since we began to develop deep feelings towards one another, we started dating. I recall telling him from the start that I would never feel sorry for him being in a wheelchair, and to see how it went. He loved the bluntness and he never wished to be seen that way. We shared a beautiful time together, as short as it was, it is a memory forever engraved upon my heart. It is amazing what he could do with his tongue and mouth, and he had no problem in directing me, into playful position, and our kissing was off the chart. The details private and yes, we had fun experimenting sexually. We talked about what it would mean in the future, my life, our life together and I made the decision, right for me at the time, and chose to step away. It was painful, and it hurt deeply as we both realised how we mirrored one another in every way. We were falling in love with one another.

A few weeks later, I received a tragic phone call that he had gone into hospital to have his shunt fitted, and there was a complication.

He developed meningitis and had died.

I was in shock, devastated and the only thing that brought inner peace was that he was now free, no longer a prisoner inside his paralysed body. He would have loved this book, and I can still hear him saying "For fuck sake, you put your fingers any closer to my mouth and I'm going to bite or suck them, 'til they drop off.". He had a strong Geordie accent, and was a soul never forgotten. Until we meet again beautiful soul. I miss your spirit; I feel you with me always. I was learning to let go and live for the now.

I would escape my Nursing as much as possible and would drive fifty miles away to hang out with friends over a weekend who were DJ's. I never fit in, was deemed weird, and Bristol felt like home.

We would dance, go on adventures, fun missions and I would spend hours drawing and even embarked upon embroidery. These people felt like my soul family, who truly got me. Creativity, music and dancing was a key to my soul and spirit. We travelled to Europe on a DJ tour, a girlfriend and I tagging along to support and be the dance crew.

We went for a month camping at a music festival. It was so much fun, we felt limitless and free. We escaped some close shaves, and all I can say is, we had our Angels on our side, guiding and protecting us from danger.

LIFE'S BLUEPRINT

<u>Wild Expression</u>

We pushed the edges of possibility

Limitless and indestructible

A group of carefree kids

Expressing our passions of music and dance

Living our daytime within a trance

Living for the weekends

To be free again

Pushing the limits of society.

Some daring and pushing the limits

Oblivious to consequences

Feeling limitless and careless

Some dicing with death

Feeling invincible

Seeking within.

Jumping on Pogo sticks

Playful expression

Being chased by security

While laughing away

BREAKING FREE

Bouncing the aisles

Pushing the boundaries

Of normal reality

Being free again.

Our inner wild

Free expression

The illusion of the noise

Mind-free drug haze

Thinking we were invincible

Reality and judgments

Worlds apart

Dancing with destiny

In a world of our own

Never sleeping from dusk to dawn

Living on the edge of time.

Many hours creating art

With our bodies

On canvas and tapestry

Weaving our expressions

Live DJ sets like no other

LIFE'S BLUEPRINT

No regrets as I explored the depths

Universe supporting this parallel reality

Achieving the impossible with no thought

No thought of failure

Belief in our hearts

The unruly and wild

Expressive and free.

Dancing for hours

Creative expression

Top DJ line up 50

With only free will in our hearts

The time of the 90's

The start of the rave scene

The trailblazers of freedom

Unique-free expression

The white gloves

A tribe of dancers

Gathering in nature

Communing together

One love tribe

Being free again!

I found soul peace in the music, a key to my spirit was dancing for hours rolled into days, over a long weekend. Parties outdoors in nature, in the middle of nowhere that would go on for days and days. Being in nature and expressing my body through movement was soothing for my soul. I felt wild, free and in a space of universal love. Taking drugs did another thing; they lifted the veil on the illusion of life, and I started to see another world outside the box of reality. It was a world of unlimited possibilities and it was a fun world of self-exploration. As a creative soul LSD opened my mind and imagination within another dimension where time and space had no relevance.

I started to see the creative inner child emerging, through dance and the hours of colouring and drawings created at the after party. I liked myself when I was on another plane of reality, as I looked happy and felt free from self-judgement. I was also connecting with deep passions and free expression.

To help you understand, the best way to describe it is like this: I felt so out of control and lost on the inside within the illusion, that when I was taken into an expanded reality, I felt free and in control. This may be hard for many to understand; it is the best way to describe the feeling of my inner world.

To experience another reality, gave me the possibility that there was more than the blinkered view of the world, I was living within. This opened my eyes to the Maya we were being fed in society!

My reactions at the time on drugs were lightning fast and in a state of flow. That is not what people think and yes it can be either way, it was almost like, I was ten-steps ahead; think 'The Matrix'. Imagine things are moving fast, yet it is in slow motion. Thankfully, I have now tapped into that state without the influence of drugs and the finetuning of my mind. As a Shaman, I have used 'psilocybin' or magic mushrooms – known to be an ancient medicinal plant – in small doses.

These create experiences that shift perception, mood and thought. With any drug, there is no safe level of use, and may carry a risk. Yet when it comes to medicinal plants, nature holds many of the keys to unlocking our inner wisdom. I now chose to be drug-free and expand a world beyond the beyond.

I have no regrets with the partying lifestyle, it was a part of my journey unfolding, and dancing was a time to express freedom. A natural inspire for others to be the best they can be, no matter their circumstances.

I wrote this following poem to empower all who have been impacted by rape, it is time to be free. You may not yet see things as I do, it is all a process and there are different phases when it comes to trauma. I am not expressing the acute phases of trauma in rape. This requires specialised and specific tender loving care. This is to break-free of the trauma that is still being carried around and the attachment to an old story. Reach out, if after years, this is still impacting your life! May this shine some light upon the dark aspects of life.

To Be Free

The walls all around me
Are closing in
To see I get to create
All from within
To step into my power
To know love from hate.

No matter what happens
I choose my fate
We each can shift
To be free from the illusion
That we each cultivate.

I chose my path with no one to blame
Now free of the bondage bullshit game of shame
The cards I was dealt perfect for this transition
With nothing but courage
To discover my soul mission

LIFE'S BLUEPRINT

From losing my sanity to losing my friends
I found myself existing within those four walls
Watching my life from the bottom of a well
It was dark, damp and scary as hell
I realised how closed off I was from the world,
sI tarted to climb up the slippery edges of hell
Hope in my heart I waved goodbye to my well.
I enjoyed the attention of living in pain
The hopeless, helpless endless emotional drain.

With worthlessness and reliable shame
The "poor me" game
The worn-out story of the victim
I played her well
Creating my internal living hell

All was created within my mind
The wall of perfection playing the game
For I had the power
Yet gave it away
The stubborn ego
Getting in the way

BREAKING FREE

My will overpowered

My virginity taken

Used and abused

A sacred offering forced upon

With no signs of remorse

The once fighter now gone

No longer fighting

Her soul frozen deep within

Overpowered by men

Manipulating my honour

Who took without asking?

And hurt me within

I forgive all and set my soul free

I took back my power victorious me

As a sovereign being

I saw past it all

I chose the perfect path

To experience it all

LIFE'S BLUEPRINT

The colouring of my tapestry
The scars of survival
A heart that is healing
I embrace them all

To now stand tall
A proud survivor
All teachers in disguise
I attracted them all
No more victim of circumstance
I welcome it all

For I am the almighty
The creator of my path
Guided by God
Love in my heart
A Spirit Warrior who knows the truth
To love all beings with no separation
No victimisation

BREAKING FREE

To be forever free
Is an individual choice
We are each given life lessons
to the pain and the humility

To dissolve hate into understanding
Judgement into misunderstanding
Sadness into joy
And find the pleasure and
make peace with the illusion of pain

I care not for what others think
As I've always been weird
I care about well-being
My voice being heard
By living my truth

I am far from perfect
I've done my time
Healed many a lifetime
Now it is time
For my spirit to shine.

I landed my first real Nursing job in Surrey, England at a small Hospital and started work as an RN (Registered Nurse) on a Gynaecology ward. I had an interest in female health and being an advocate for healthy choices around sensuality.

I was taken under the wing of an amazing nurse who infused much passion into her teachings. During this time, I met some amazing people. I recall meeting an incredibly special soul who was a Nun, and I was invited over for tea and scones, of which I enjoyed. I began to see, that no matter our religion, in a safe space of love, kindness and acceptance, we are all equal and loved by God. We can shift beyond beliefs and meet soul to soul.

During this time, I was passing out on the anti-depressant medication mixed with alcohol and hash. You know you are in a bad way when your boyfriend finds you passed out, having defecated on the rug and more than once wet yourself from the passing out. It is sad to think back, and end chapters that are now closed, with love. You get the picture, a soul who is lost, scared and drowning on the inside. Even though I was lost inside, I began to feel a sense of belonging in my new role. I was proud to be a Nurse and progressed up the ladder swiftly. Expanding upon skills such as Phlebotomy, insertion of intravenous cannulas, and running in-service training for other nurses. I felt a passion for teaching arising deep within, and after my six months there I left to travel to Australia, with my boyfriend at the time.

COMING HOME

I came to Australia at 27-years young. I waved goodbye to Mum and knew I was never coming back. Shaved off all my hair to a number two, was wild with a rebellious girl attitude. I was giving off a persona of fearlessness and bad ass, yet on the inside, I was screaming out to feel loved. It was time to leave and recreate the new me – a fresh start. I felt like I was finally coming home.

I was running from myself and deep into another destructive abusive and toxic relationship. I am grateful to have got out the country in one piece, as the two weeks before I left, I was a tornado in self-destruct.

Wow, reversing up a one-way street on a rainy day, shouting out to my friend and crashing my car into a learner driver. Almost getting arrested for jumping the train on the way to London to get my visa, and then passing out on a bus whilst listening to The Cure. To be awoken at the other end of the bus line and flipping out as I thought I was being attacked. It took four police to hold me down, I had a flashback to the rape, and thought I was being hurt, yet I was fighting on the inside.

I had a toxic-potion of anti-depressants in my bloodstream, mixed with alcohol; they thought I was on PCP, as I went into fight-mode, a fear response to stress. I was placed into a police cell for my own safety, and for hours I kicked the door with my feet and fists. I did not like being caged, yet it was 'I' who was living in my own inner hell of soul suffocation.

Thinking back to this is scary and sad to think of the darkness I was existing within. There was 20 years of bottled up anger, frustration, rejection, self-hate, and rage that was coming out. I was imploding and I had no idea how to manage it and was rejecting life. What would follow would be more years of suppression and doing anything to numbing out the pain. I thought of leaving this out, as it's a crazy picture, yet I see this happen to teenage girls / boys, and young adults, often after a dodgy drug and a toxic mixing of prescription medications with alcohol.

So yes, anyone and everyone can shift, when they are guided with kindness, unconditional love and compassion. The individual must see it, as awareness is brought into their reality and a path to inner healing, which is about learning to love yourself and working through the pain.

Following my arrival in Queensland, I experienced a violent run in with my boyfriend, this story is expressed in the poem below. I learned how to surf and spent much time on the beaches. I really enjoyed the shift to working in Australia, and truly feeling part of a healthcare team. There are very fond memories of the doctor's parties and the adventures that were shared.

Stop Fighting Within

Coming to Australia,

Well-awaited fresh start

Time to recreate

An improvement of my life.

I shaved off all my hair

To a number two

A fresh identity a social statement

My inner reality of sadness and pain.

Connecting with my sister

From years apart

I'd missed her presence within my heart

Started off with learning to surf

Single fin board

Camping on rugged beaches

Shark signs all new to me

Beautiful secluded beaches

Fearless within

A special soul Friend of my sister's family

Taught me how to surf

A wild spirit and forever young

LIFE'S BLUEPRINT

In heart and soul

Who has now passed at 58,

Forever gone in body

Exploring new adventures

His memory and spirit lives on

Living with depression

Numbed out on medication

I chased escapism from my own reality

Weed expansion and free of thought

Found pockets of clarity in my heart

Fought demons within my mind

Feeling soothed by the ocean waves

Sitting within nature

A new-found church waited in my heart

In a relationship from overseas

Became co-dependent in every way

Supporting us both as a nurse

Not the ideal shift I had hoped for, that's for sure.

BREAKING FREE

A moment of unconsciousness

We both cracked one night

With drugs on board

Our perceptions blurred

Clarity colliding

Attacking one another

Lost in our hearts

Hurting one another

Never backing down from the fists that flew

My teeth bit down in defence

Tearing at flesh

Protecting my face

I am not proud of my animalistic wild response

Fighting like dogs lost in a haze

Never backing down until cold on the floor

Coming off worse blackout into submission silent within.

We chose to step away for good

Both fearful for it getting much worse

Our love turned sour

Morphed into hate
I found my inner strength
Before something else sealed my fate
To step away for good
On another journey
To find and love myself.

Any relationship, where creativity is not expressed or nourished will lead to destructive behaviour, and it takes only one to wake-up, step up, and walk away. Learn the lesson then move on. It was three months later that I ventured into the Australian Outback, a deeply spiritual and grounding place to re-group. This was one of the most amazing experiences working as a nurse and gave me a deep sense of the Spirit of Australia and the beautiful Aboriginal culture. There are many stories there that shifted my perspective to life, put it this way, life was never dull.

LOOSING MYSELF

"Creativity unexpressed is a destructive path, I had to be the change within."

In reflection I became a Nurse as I wanted to help people; yet on the inside I needed to help myself. It made me feel wanted and worthy as a person at the time. I was also brought up in a household where medical topics were discussed over the dinner table and finding dead animals to dissect was the norm.

Nursing was a great profession as it gave me my plane ticket and a way to live in Australia, of which I am grateful, as without it, writing this book and following my passions would have been a struggle. Sadly, many people build their self-worth and personal value on their career. This was so far from my natural essence.

As a coach, I will throw a rope to another to catch, but they must be willing to grab it; I am more of an inspirator and uplifter. When I was a nurse, I was helping others as it made me feel good and worthy inside. I wanted to empower others to shift as I loved health promotion and education in my nursing role, it was a key to my path to be revealed.

It was years later whilst living in Sydney, working as a Nurse that life would deliver another big lesson. This is just the tip of the iceberg...

A big wake-up call.

It was one foggy morning on the way to work as an RN, and there was a tragic and life-changing road fatality.

I was the driver.

The details are private out of respect for the beautiful 18-year old soul and his family. What I can say is he had allegedly been beaten up, put on the road, and left there. It all happened so fast, and it plays in slow motion within my mind if I go there; this was 19-years ago. I got to experience the shock that drivers go through following an accident, and how they drive off at the scene. They are in shock, fight or flight mode, where the rational part of the mind shuts down, and the reptilian brain is in full force. I recall attempting to drive my car, my legs shaking, bouncing on the pedals after my car landed post-impact, in shock.

I am forever grateful to the man walking his dog, who stopped me from running over to the scene; he told me that it was a body I had hit. I wanted to go over, he thankfully held me back, the shock began to hit me, and the rest was a blur. I was taken to the police station to be questioned and interviewed, my life hung in the balance, as tragically one life was taken too soon.

My family were in the UK, my mum flew over to give me the emotional support I needed, and to be held with nourishment. I hit rock bottom, diagnosed with PTSD *(post-traumatic stress disorder)*, with recurring flashbacks, I was on hyper alert, even the slightest noise would send me into a downward spiral. I was in disbelief, it was surreal, and as I write this it still feels like yesterday. I was learning the preciousness and fragility of life. Each year I would remember his soul, my body would remember, and then it would hit me left field, every year. Until April 2018 when it was finally released.

This poem I wrote to guide myself through the dark moments in July 2017, to remember the light within, as it was the anniversary of his passing. This was one of the most painful releases.

No hiding I opened publicly and reached out to be supported on digital social media. I am grateful to now be in a peaceful place of love, and that this trauma no longer comes up.

A Soul Taken Too Soon

The past is the past

After 17 years

the scars remained

Traumatic events, may pass

The pain body never forgets.

I am unsure of the words to express

Tears fall, and I let go again

Each year, it comes.

Hits me smack bang in the face,

Depths once hidden away

Come up as I release some more.

Why am I the way I am?

I get this question every day?

Others see the light and the love,

Yet the darker depths, I hide away.

Trusting they will heal in time

Each year at this time

They come up, bang, another layer.

LIFE'S BLUEPRINT

For a time, my own life uncertain
Hung in the balance,
A life lost and my life at a cross roads
Freedom almost taken away,
Locked away, freedom denied
A new directed destined path.

Given another chance,
To live a free life and journey of healing
To never waste another breath
To find myself within the mess,
It didn't' happen overnight,
Yet, I never gave up the fight
To uncover my soul mission.

Another layer of the pain,
Trauma so deep, I weep each year
A beautiful soul, so young
Taken too soon.
An unconscious disconnected action
A road fatality, it's all a blur
Scenes of tragedy happened so fast.

BREAKING FREE

To continue to live each day.
As if it's my last.
To keep letting go of the past
To forgive my unconsciousness,
Moment of blindness, a massive 'wake-up'
Yet carry him forever within my heart
To never play small, ever again.

Each day is precious,
You never know what is coming,
Love at 111% or nothing at all,
It is time to raise the bar,
Fuck mediocrity and complacency.
Be here now, or not at all.

Savour every breath, as if it's your last
Love those so deep, as if it's the last
Speak those words of truth and love
Tell those you love, open your hearts,
Never sacrifice honouring your truth

LIFE'S BLUEPRINT

The fragility of life, taken so soon,
I ask you to hold your hearts,
Be my courage and guiding hands.
Open your hearts as you are the light,
To light a candle for those you adore
Souls take too young and way too soon
Remember them and choose to live on.

It's only for a few days
Then I'll be right, to walk alone.
Shining with love and forever so bright,
It's part of my mission, to be the light
To guide others to safety
So, they may save themselves
I am sorry; I couldn't save your life.

A quality and gift I have learnt from an early age is trying to turn around a bad situation, like making lemonade from lemons. We are each going through our own lessons in the journeys of life, so we can each discover the cause to then create a different effect. How we see something is a choice, and learning to act, rather than a lifetime of reactions. So many souls beat themselves up in shame and guilt daily. There is a lesson within lessons ready to be revealed, about you. I live my life with passion, and for more than one life.

My spirit is here to be expressed, as so too is yours! So, if you are stuck in a situation and not living with passion, then why not? I desire for everyone to live the best life ever, no matter what we have experienced, as we all deserve it.

No matter the adversity, we can all find inner freedom.

I learnt that most things are out of our control; the bigger picture of all involved, we are unable to see or know.

A second later, a different reaction at the time, may have created a very different reality, and from what I learned was, had I made another split-second decision and action I may not be here to share the story. Another life, gone too young. I was given another chance.

When a traumatic event occurs, the body and soul needs attention, guidance and space to heal. This may take months or even years. It is a journey of the soul.

During those years and around the time of the trauma, bodybuilding gave me a focus, and became an important factor to finding my way home. It channelled my emotions, ignited inner confidence to function and directed energy into constructive creativity. I was still hiding the self-punishment of bulimia, was battling low self-esteem, yet was able to function in the world and achieve set goals.

Relationships Teach

Co-dependency seemed to be the flavour

My inner world and projection of self

This time shaded with jealousy and insecurity

The wounded feeding off one another

Searching for love to feel complete

Never feeling full and seeking more

While feeling even more empty within.

It never started off this way

A love connection appears so deep

A common denominator as if you are made for one another

A gentle soul and we trained together

Always by one another's side

Thinking it was forever!

As I started to grow, his jealousy increased

I sculpted my body and transformed within

The chameleon getting attention again

My confidence blossoming

Passion of body sculpting and nutrition

BREAKING FREE

A love of the sweaty bodybuilding gym
I gained the respect and attention
From other pumped up iron men.

They became my support system
Having my back, encouraging me to compete
And move away from lack
The addiction of discipline
Of challenging my resolve
I loved the buzz and passion from deep within.

They were like brothers
I had longed for from a child
Nourishing my spirit and inner strength
Respecting my feminine presence
My wild inner essence
Masculine presence was grounding
Took under their wing with loving guidance.

Everyone you meet is a teacher you see
A simple reflection of what is within

LIFE'S BLUEPRINT

Know when it is time to step away
Rather than fighting and
Losing more of you along the way
The details are irrelevant
The lessons learnt
We stepped away for good.

To know what you desire from deep within
A man who is confident
Masculine and true in his presence
A magnetic pull from deep inside
A man you admire and adore
Instant attraction
Yet unavailable.
To be only friends

You both joke as he, your brother
His little sister he adores
Feeling drawn to one another
Another lifetime
Sweet moments in time perhaps?

So, the journey continues

An evolution within

To stay true on you path

Resisting the temptation

With self-respect and honesty intact

Letting go of the fantasy

The school girl crush

Where your heart flips with his name

Entire body rush.

To let go even more

To continue to grow

In your own unique way

A new direction

A lifelong friendship

That is enough

We choose our path.

I was competing with body fat dangerously low, and developed amenorrhea for six months. I placed last in a category where the women were fuller and maintained their femininity (figure class). Had I been in the bodybuilding (physique) category, the judges said I would have placed first in the Nationals and gone onto the Worlds in the USA.

I really wanted to re-shape my body as the feminine form of the Figure girls had a greater appeal and was less hard to look at. The next day after my first ever bodybuilding competition, I was back in the gym, day one of the 12-month plan. The guys that trained there sent me home to rest, so I took one day off.

I was determined to re-shape and create the body I desired. I focused upon my vision and did what I set out to do. A year later I competed at the Australian Natural Bodybuilding Figure Nationals and placed second. I qualified for the Australian Team and was looking at competing at the World championships in Europe. However, they were cancelled, so I never got to compete at Worlds.

I was back training for the Nationals for the following year, I came in the best prepared I had ever been and learned a massive lesson, an insight. I placed last, which shocked many that at the end professional Bodybuilders came to share their thoughts, that I was the best up there.

That day, I started to learn that no one can judge you, as the only one judging is you. I felt the sting of political games as I had decided that year to structure my own diet, training strategy and do it my way, in a healthier way for my body, as my own coach! I learnt that in life, 'it is who you know that opens the doors.'

I tasted humility, bit back tears of disappointment and stood in my power. I was proud and performed the best I had ever done, and that is all that mattered. No trophy and when they did place the medal around my neck, I removed it, said "Thank You" and walked off the stage in front of 2,000 people. I cut the cord, another lesson in disappointment and abandonment that I was not ready to let go of.

Shaping my body at this high level of training taught me:

- A willingness to keep looking forward
- Strength of character
- Persistence - to never stay down
- Discipline to practice
- To be, do and having anything I desire
- Focus
- Determination
- Mastery in will
- Chose healthier choices

I am grateful for it all, from all that I learned and who I became as a result.

2001 NSW State ANB National Figure Contest

BREAKING FREE

At thirty I was diagnosed with arthritis in my left knee and would be looking at a procedure called a Tibial Osteotomy if I kept running and training hard. I decided to find a cure to the arthritis as I had pain, and every day my knee was swollen.

I relocated to Queensland to be near to my family. About twelve months later while working in the Emergency Department, a patient spat in my face; he was hepatitis C positive. Blood was taken and when my baseline blood test came back, I was given some shocking news: "You are HIV positive".

I returned to work in a daze of shock; I went into autopilot, my logical brain in a state of inner confusion. I was carrying on like a robot and felt numbness take over my entire being. I felt in a different plane of existence, and suddenly, I went into panic and reaction mode. I could not breath and had to get out of there.

A moment held in time and the disbelief of why is this happening to me?

I left what I was doing, handed over to a nurse, saying, "I have to leave". I ran into my manager's office, burst into tears and screamed through choking tears, "I have HIV, I have to go home".

She was amazing beyond words, through sobs and choking back the screams I told her about the blood results. My boyfriend picked me up, I called my sister and then went and hung out with her, we drank wine, and both decided it could be worse, as I could have diabetes.

We turned a very dark outlook into a positive one. We hugged, laughed nervously and cried together. She rang the hospital the next day and spoke to the infectious diseases unit and they re-ran the test.

Two days later they rang to say that it was a false positive.

Relief does not even come close to how I felt; we celebrated. I was clear! Yes, a false result.

The human psyche is interesting, as many of you will have only heard the words 'HIV' and 'positive', and your own fears kicking in. It is like going to the doctors and jumping to the worst-case scenario. This will tell you much about the way you live your life. Yes, having a false positive happens!

Wow, big wake-up!

Three months later, while working in the Emergency Room, a female patient in the mental health lock up room charged at the door. I was standing in the line of fire, and she punched me in the face. I ended up with a fractured cheek bone and a small fracture of the periorbital eye socket. It was then my body and mind went into total shut down mode.

I was diagnosed with *Depression and Anxiety Stress Disorder.*

I was medicated on two types of anti-depressants and was functionally unable to work for three months. It was time to sort things out for good. I was photographed by forensics and a legal case was commenced. The hearing did not come about until years later, when I was pregnant with our first child; I dropped all charges, forgave the patient and learnt the lesson - to move on with my amazing life. I recall depression feeling like being at the bottom of a well and simply existing. I would sit there and watch the world go by. Where did I fit in? I felt like a fuck-up, a misfit, changing my sense of identity many times as I wanted to find my 'fit' in a group. I had two choices: sit there and rot or start climbing up and get my life back - that is what I did. I fell many times, slipped back, yet I never gave up.

I had lost my friends, and my family were getting weary of my games. No one was going to do it for me. It was a process and all about baby steps to recovery.

Once back at work, I decided to reduce my medication, though my GP wanted me to stay on them. I felt numb, like I was flat lining my emotions. I reduced them myself and started to feel highs and lows of my emotions again. To feel the reality of living free and not numb, ever again. This was another wake-up and my recovery guided me down the path, and to the perfect journey back to begin healing myself, to break free.

I recall going to my first ever yoga retreat in Australia, and it was there that I did my first ever yoga class, learnt about Reiki and started the 'onion effect' journey of removing the many layers created over time. Initially I was excited to go, then the day came, and while being driven there, I started popping anti-depressants like they were lollies. I was punching myself in the head with my fists in the car, to numb the internal pain as I was overcome with absolute panic and fear.

I was about to look at my stuff, and there would be stuff to address. I felt powerless and was shit fucking scared!

Let us be honest and candid here, it takes courage and a big push to start to look at your stuff. It is so much easier to blame others. I was so attached to my story, my sense of self, who I thought I was, and I had built upon it, thinking "who am I without my story?" I thought I was the product of it. I was about to have my ego exposed.

As I arrived, I recall looking at everyone and my mind was in judgement mode and high jacked by comparisons. I saw everyone else as having their shit together. They looked happy and were mingling around the table. I felt disconnected, my posture slumped forward in shame and thinking, 'I am not worthy to be here'. I felt uncomfortable like everyone was staring at me and I was shaking inside and out. As everyone around the table introduced themselves, playing a game to recall what the others had said, by the time it was my turn my brain went blank and I felt awkward. I think I was shaking and close to tears, frozen in panic.

Day two arrived and I was still on the outside of my body and not in it. Does that make sense? I felt like a robot going through the motions an emotional train wreck, very exposed and feeling uncomfortable. I was vulnerable and emotionally disconnected. The Reiki Master pulled me aside and offered some healing using acupuncture needles. I said yes, what did I have to lose. He proceeded to place some needles into my body. I felt some calm come into my body, a new feeling of letting go. He said you have much anger in your body. Wow, it started to make sense, tears started to roll down my cheeks, I was so angry at the world, my life and feeling like I never fitted in. Then the entire liver area on the skin turned black. I had another big emotional release and cried, there had been so much disappointment in my life, sadness, anger, loss and times of powerlessness, it all started to flood out.

That weekend was a big shift in the right direction as I started to allow some of the layers to be released. I would do much hip opening work and many times would cry on my yoga mat as I released. I went home smiling and had a glimpse of what love and oneness would feel like. The layers began to dissolve, slowly.

Are you starting to see beyond the biological-physical to address the root cause of the symptoms?

I started to surf and get in the ocean as much as I could, with Reiki healing sessions in a group every week, and I also started my yoga journey on the mat. I was drawn more to Pilates at the time, as later I went on to teach it. Healing is a journey all on its own. Your body will only release what it is ready to release; there is no force, no pushing against your nervous system, as it needs time to re-adjust and re-wire. So be gentle and allow the resting into expansion after the letting go.

The ego will hide at all cost.

The greatest journey is reclaiming you, and it is also the most challenging.

From my story I hope that you start to see that all the things that happen or have happened, have all been created from the unconscious thought patterns and old programs of behaviours. They may also be contracts that you made before coming into this lifetime, to clear up karma and learn valuable life lessons from. It taught me that some of us are here to walk that path alone as a leader, as a change maker. There is no place to fit in, and all to embrace as a free spirit.

"No one deserves adversity, and no one wants traumatic things to happen. Yet, it may be a vital aspect of the journey back to self." Zoe Bell

I have realised that in some professions they do not like the people that are different. The ones that have fresh passion are stubborn and unable to be moulded and manipulated into obedient sheep. The leaders of change are depicted as the troublemakers, it goes way back in history.

In 2005 at age 34 enjoying yoga practice at ocean's edge

In Western medicine we look at the physical layer – at symptom control, but this does not uncover the root cause of the disease, illness or ailment to inner healing and self- discovery.

I started re-exploring my sexuality with women, and the softness was safe and loving when I would go out to clubs, especially the kissing and also the attention and power I felt with it. The men could watch but not join in. It was hot, and it was a form of control, feeling powerful and blatant manipulation. I was finding a way to feel empowered again, yet this was powerlessness in disguise, as I was giving up my self-worth and was disconnected with the self. I started to manipulate my sexuality with power, which fed on the internal unworthiness and lack of self-love. I liked the softness and gentleness of women, as it felt safe and the kissing was sensual. I was going through normal self-exploration and freedom to be curious.

I tasted a deep spiritual connection, yet his path was set, and he came in as fast as he left. The vital message to give me was, 'You need to read this book, go and find the book'. At the time I was dancing off my face on ecstasy and looking very free yet lost within. The book was 'The Celestine Prophecy'. This book has a life all of its own and is another story! The seed was planted. As I began to read the book, then the same insights came into my life. This is how a friend described the first edition to this book, he said at times it became so intense, he had to put it down until he had processed the words. So, if you need to read this in stages, then honour your inner guidance.

It was around the age of thirty-three, when I started to attend personal development events, I recall being pulled aside by a beautiful man and healer who described my energy of rushing around in a crazy eights, highs and lows like a tornado. He saw my energy, that I was unaware of at the time. My body was worked on over two ninety-minute sessions. It was like an exorcism of the dark and stuck sexual energy that was trapped deep within my pelvis.

There was an entity within my body that had been feeding off me and the low vibration I was running at. It was full of fear, hate and sadness. The entity was sucking the life-force out of me, draining my energy and inner sparkle. As it was being drawn out of my body, I was shaking, overcome with waves of panic as the entity was coiled around my spine and hiding within my pelvic area. It was being drawn out through my body and up to my throat. I was overcome with a choking feeling, like a massive ball of wool was being drawn out of my body. The fear within was pulling it back down, I had to laugh crazily and laugh more. I was crying, sobbing, choking and laughing through salty tears. It was intense, and waves of anger came up, I had to be courageous and strong.

As this thing left my body out through my throat, there was a blowing noise all around me, ancient tribal noises and much laughing, it was very tribal.

More emotions released as it came out, I gasped for air and released some more, where I eventually passed out and slept for a solid two hours. It was exhausting, and my body was taking over, when rest comes, go with it, know when to surrender!

I attended other personal development seminars and at one of them there was process where we accessed our subconscious mind. As I came out of the process, I gazed up in a room of 3,000 people, my eyes met with another and I felt overcome with the thought, "I need him", and had a burning desire to speak with him, it was the strangest thing, like I was under a magic spell. He was the one on stage. The subconscious realm is a very personal sacred space, so when I work with clients in the meditation, once the powerful process begins, I avoid any eye contact. When working with intimacy, the eyes are the doorway to the soul, and safe boundaries must be established.

I was to learn valuable lessons and gain insights into what I found attractive in a man. A man with charisma, living his passion and successful was desirable. I also learnt that a man with honesty and integrity outweighed charisma and charm by far, and he was my teacher of Self.

The lessons: disappointment, rejection and abandonment.

I believed in the fantasy. It was around the time of my dad passing away. I also came to the realisation that life is a game of choices and consequences, and we both were sexually attracted to one another. I see this soul with deep love, honour and respect. I am grateful to opening my eyes into an expanded reality.

I felt disappointment stacked upon disappointment around relationships with men, and abandonment kicked in big time. I remember the deep conversations with my dad, the weeks before he passed away. He wanted to know why I had not found the right man and married, he wondered if I would ever meet him and have children.

I told Dad, at the right time he will find me, and we would one day have children. I guess he was also trying to figure out how two daughters can be so different when it came to meeting 'the one', sharing love, having a family, and seeing us happy in this regard.

A seed was planted that day, deep within my subconscious mind. I felt lost after Dad died and went back on a sure path of self-destruct. It was a short-lived self-destruct as something shifted, and life took a beautiful pause. A short relationship/friendship developed with a beautiful man, who was ten years older than me. He was living his passion, travelling the world, photographing beautiful naked women and doing what he loved in exotic places. This was instrumental to following my heart.

Most mornings we shared a beach walk, many times hanging out with his dad, who introduced me to many ancient aspects of yoga. This was a very grounding and nourishing time for me. After saying goodbye to my dad, I found much comfort in spending time with two beautiful gentle souls with the perfect male energy, it was lots of fun.

He steered me towards Anthony Robbins, I started to read more Personal Development books and that year I attended my first Anthony Robbins event, 'Date with Destiny' a six-day intensive. This changed my life. I started to see into the masks and games I had been playing, and more of the layers of the onion started to peel away, for clarity and insight to be revealed. It was the perfect teaching for that time in my life.

Life would never be the same again.

It would be at Date with Destiny, that I would align with a beautiful man, my rock and the father of our children. Life was happening so fast, and it was a powerful time, where a piece of my father's soul chose to come back.

It was in early 2019, just before Jakes 12th birthday, that I would realise that it would be this lifetime, that he had been my father and now was our son. The topic of Soul family is magical to unravel, as I know that Charlie, our youngest, has also been my brother in another lifetime. Life is beautiful and both these souls have a powerful mission, as themselves, in their own unique way.

<u>Perfect Time of Calling Out</u>

At a time of asking

A beautiful Soul entered my life

A knight in shining armour

Blessed our lives.

The details not relevant

For this story

A piece of the puzzle to be left unknown

Not my stone to over-turn

The bigger purpose for co-creation

Of two magical souls

Two boys who blessed our hearts

Enriched our lives for the best.

Change is inevitable in life

We grow together

Or we grow apart

I felt lost inside

LIFE'S BLUEPRINT

My desires changed
From having everything
A home, family, materialistic gifts
I let go of the dream
And did the unthinkable
I had an affair
To feel free and alive again
I desired a spiritual connection
A karmic lesson
To forgive the past and heal
The inner child within.

I recall the pain within my children
Falling apart inside
What had I had created
All to be free and alive from within
An illusion and fearful escapism
From taking responsibility
To step away cleanly
I was the coward

BREAKING FREE

Rather than hurt others
Driving a dagger into my rocks back
The father of my children
Shaking our family apart

The man who chose to stand beside me
Till death us do part
On the inside, I felt trapped in a box.
I chose to not catch the guilt and shame

A colouring of my past tapestry
It was time to step up and own it
In all its raw pain
Community gossip projected shame
To stand tall with my head held high
Be true to myself and step away

To love the inner child inside
Hold her close and nurture her pain
To now be the adult
For my child looking for guidance

LIFE'S BLUEPRINT

To be their guiding light with
Only love in my heart
To forgive my actions and
By not listening to my intuition
Restore our family home security and home in tatters
Of disharmony and pain
It wasn't easy,
I'll say that much I wore the bad parent
Caught the words that cut like a knife

Each time picking myself up
And falling apart I found myself in another living hell
Everything I didn't ever want
I had created it all
The life of the single parent.

We found our way through the jungle
Tangled emotions, minefields of trauma
Both taking responsibility for respecting one another
To heal lifetimes of karma
To break the chain of dysfunction

BREAKING FREE

A great father, caring man
Our children have done well.

Our lives are like chapters in a book
No right or wrong and no one to blame
It is about falling, growing and learning
We chose our family as part of our soul path.

Maybe from the contrast to dive deeper into our hearts
My life growing up was never normal
So why would it be normal now?
We are a two-parent family
Living apart.

I am happy
I followed my heart
Now I am walking a spiritual path
I found my way back to self
The greatest gift of all, is love.

Giving birth was the most empowering experience as a woman, with the spiritual transition into motherhood. My vagina would expand as it needed to, and I trusted in the wisdom of my body. I really shifted in womanhood by giving birth, I said it would be like having a massive orgasm as I breathed our babies out. We each have a unique journey!

Jake's journey would begin with his cord around his neck, blue and requiring resuscitation in the bath, while I held him. He was taken to the baby unit, where very shortly after we were able to hold him. A special beautiful soul came into the world, as we feel in love with him. I recall him in my arms and thinking, Wow, I am responsible for another soul now. This is the most important role I will ever have, to be taking care of another being. It is an incredibly special time and one that goes by so fast. He was very independent and was walking at eight and a half months old.

Four months later, I was pregnant with our second child, Charlie, and nine months later gave birth to another beautiful soul to fall in love with. His arrival was longer, though smoother than Jake's as I was more relaxed. After thirteen hours of pushing, he finally arrived, five hours later we were home.

I waddled out as my vagina was so swollen; it was unrecognisable from all the pressure of pushing a baby out with his waters still intact! I had decided it was good luck a week before and that is what I almost got; the mind is powerful! There was no way I was stretching that much, thankfully the nurse burst my waters with her nails.

Hello, pelvic floor.

This is when my pelvic floor really woke up, after baby number two, the intensity of my orgasms increased when I masturbated and during intercourse. I suddenly knew what I was activating. They were more intense and powerful. I began to explore more fantasies in my mind.

After not listening to my intuition and deep feelings, my body sexually started to switch off. I ignored the messages for two years and was losing my ability to become naturally aroused. I had to get out as I was dying on the inside. I was longing for that deep soul spiritual connection. I had lost my voice to express my truth. It was time to be free.

Sexually I became frigid, not listening to my instinct and had no idea who I was anymore. I had an affair, which was the one thing I said I would never do. It was the thing that took me so long to get over, from the choices my dad made, yet, for the first time in a long time I felt free and alive as a woman. From feeling sexually unresponsive and emotionally switched off, with most of my attention on being a Momma, and not listening to my heart, I realised there was nothing wrong with my healthy body responses.

I had lost myself.

I had also stabbed my best friend in the back.

I had taken the coward approach as I was resisting taking responsibility for my life.

I had lost my voice, with a fear of speaking up, and was creating a mess behind me!

He made an appointment for us to see a marriage therapist.

I was carrying the secret of having an affair. I was lying to a man who loved and adored me and would do anything for me. I had hurt my best friend.

I felt lost self-respect and had no idea of whom I was. I was screaming on the inside to be honoured and respected, as a woman.

It was time to stand on my own feet and chose to start on a journey to rediscover and love me. I was sorry for creating the mess and over time that I did not have the courage to step away before. I understood that I did the one thing that I would never go back, as to ignore your intuition is to lose your soul. I am grateful as this would be the beginning of a journey of 'Breaking Free'. It was with Self.

For many years we worked towards building a relationship that is friendly and respectful, as this is vital for any children whose parents separate and go through divorce. It is humbling to reach out when you have nothing and was grateful for the support when I asked, and he has supported this transition into my soul calling, I am eternally grateful.

We cannot change the past, yet we can create a different meaning, and from my story you will see, the ego will defend itself at all cost. I let go and forgave myself for not speaking up at the time, when met with unwanted comments that were no longer aligned with my truth; there comes a time to stop reacting to the charge. Life will present opportunities to set new boundaries as empowered woman or man.

At the end of a day the way children witness their Mum and Dad treating one another, will impact their own future relationships with women and men. We have a great relationship that is healthy, respectful and a flowing sense of humour.

Let us all begin to raise the bar, and I am sure you can see, I am far from perfect. I have never seen myself as a single parent, for my children have two amazing loving parents. As long they are loved unconditionally, I am grateful. I see a beautiful man and soul who has a longing in his heart, and his boys are his Universe. They are blessed to have such a magnificent man as a guide in their life. I hope that one day he finds that romantic soul love with a beautiful soul to share his life with. As a soul, I will never suppress, ignore or silence my inner voice again.

Instinct is wisdom guiding the heart. Having said all this, the journey has been perfect for the lessons that were learnt and that I am grateful we have two beautiful, happy and healthy boys.

Dress up with my gorgeous children, for my sister's 50th birthday

With my sister, and mum on her 70th birthday

Chapter 2: Finding My Voice

"The most courageous act is still to think for yourself aloud."

– Coco Chanel

Voices In The Head

The heard is the voice in the head, the one that never switches off and the more you push it away, the louder it gets. The inner voice or inner critic was one of self-loathing, disgust and worthlessness. We all have this inner voice. The always listening, commentating noise in the head. It is always there.

Some have many of these voices, sub-personalities finding a way to be acknowledged, gaining attention in any way they can. Some are unaware of this voice, they think it is who they are, fighting against one another, and unable to listen to the one they are fighting with. It will always be right, will hide at all cost and will not want to be found out. It has kept you trapped in your mind. The eyes become blinded, and the ears become deaf.

The guilt of what you think you have done wrong, will eat you alive.

The shame of what you have made wrong, will suffocate your soul.

The blame will keep you trapped in the maze, repeating more of the same.

The voices in the head, will only begin to quieten when we teach the mind to sit still, with a disciplined practice of meditation. This daily practice is a safe place to take refuge as we safely de-clutter the stuff in the head. To acknowledge what I had created in the path of destruction was ugly and took courage. The impact this had on my children was profound, as I was shifting through my worst nightmare.

It was time to step up and take responsibility for what I had created, and create the life I desired, even though at the time I had no idea what that was. The reality was, I was playing the victim card, stuck in my story, and no fucking idea how to get out of my head. The only path to honouring this voice was to take responsibility for what I had done.

To own my truth to everything in my life.

To be accountable with those I had impacted.

To step up and take responsibility in my actions.

It took many years to reach a point where I was ready to own my voice, it is not something that happens overnight. The layers of unconsciousness run deeper than we realise, with much willingness to fall flat on your face. I still find confrontation a challenge, I am embracing each step and rising to the challenge.

It was time to ask for a teacher to guide me out of the maze.

Rarely people awaken overnight, most will require many teachers over their lifetime. To listen to the voices with nothing to come back to, a stable base and practices to stick to, is a sure path to insanity. I would have gone insane many times over, had I not had a stable base to keep coming back to. The layers of awareness are there for our protection. To stop us waking up too soon. We must navigate the path, overcoming each level of new awareness to learn to break free from the inside out.

To wake-up, to drop back into sleeping and so it continues.

There is another type of heard, the herd of voices from others. The echo of voices behind the back, the bitter remarks, the jealous taunts, the slut-haters and mummy bloggers that judge your way of being. This is an aspect that would take years to develop, to trust what was being transmitted and to allow it to pass through with minimal damage to my heart.

I would also begin to understand that this is even louder in their own minds. It was sad to think how trapped they were, stuck in rightness and wrongness. This is where the healing of the inner masculine within the feminine needs to take place. This is explored in more depth, in Wildflower – Reclaiming a Sacred Place.

I was working nights as a Registered Nurse to support my family. My self-esteem a mess, functioning on little to no sleep, and was unable to say No! to sexual advances from men. My word 'no' meant nothing, battling deep shame, guilt and self-loathing from my actions and inability to keep my word. I ignored my intuition and gave in to a man who kept pushing to connect. He would bring me the perfect lesson, as a few months later I found out that I had the Herpes Simplex Virus.

All disease – I believe – is created within the mind and the blocks that we have yet to let go and learn to love.

I eliminated the Herpes virus from my body and have gone on to guide many others towards this powerful process. This is explored in detail in Chapter 6: Soul Freedom from Entrapment. It is the beliefs that are within the subconscious part of the mind that shape the way we see the world, and the voices in our heads that reinforce these limiting beliefs. We each create the perfect scenario, so we can heal, release the old beliefs and grow into the beautiful beings that we are.

Our thoughts and beliefs create our reality.

The Universe delivered the perfect teacher, a beautiful Jamaican soul would enter our life. After calling out, down on my knees looking up at the sky, tears streaming down my face in overwhelm screaming.

FINDING MY VOICE

Is this fucking it!

He heard my cries. He was looking for the student to teach and pass on all this ancient Vedic wisdom. He was also learning about relationship within Self. As I began the daily practices of the meditation and ancient wisdom, I began to find the courage to express my truth, and eventually stop lying, to myself and everyone else in my life. I was exposed, raw and humble. This opened a door to learning to love the aspects I had shamed and unveiled my passions, it unleashed my voice, and the courage to teach others.

"Life is about living your truth while having the courage to be disliked."

One of the keys to my success, to step into this powerful and confident woman was the Vedic / Transcendental meditation, he guided me through. It was boot camp Zoe101 and I am forever grateful for his take-no-victims approach, to finally put down the victim crap, shift my attitude, heal my inner child and reclaim my family life. There was no hiding, he saw, smelled and sensed it all. The games, the masks, the manipulation, and as I asked all was given. I had to learn how to fall in love with me. Unless we each have a stable base to return to, change can feel like you are drowning.

The path of the warrior is not a bed of roses, it's tough and exposing. No matter what else was going on, the meditation practice became the smooth elixir to my sanity. The daily relief from the chaos, a resting experience for the mind created all these offerings below.

- To love the diamond in the rough
- To learn to love self
- Own my doo-doo (stuff)
- Step into my power
- Find my voice to honour my 'No!'
- Awaken my confidence.
- Rewire my mind
- Stand in my own truth
- Rise above the herd
- Forgive in a heartbeat
- Iron out the BS games
- Evoked a tantric embodiment
- Creativity unleashed with poetry and books published
- A passion for presenting on camera
- To living my dream life.

I am passionate about this as I wonder how many women and men are living like this every day, with this too as their reality. Feeling trapped in how they feel with a large piece of the 'communication' puzzle missing. They have forgotten their own inner voice and for far too many they are not being respected, heard or honoured. This is a path to breaking free of co-dependent relationships for both men and women.

Within the pockets of stillness from the daily discipline of doing the inner work, there comes the space for an inner voice of wisdom and intuition to come through. It is the over powerful out of control ego that will keep you trapped within your mind and is the main villain of being able to break free. Teachers will come and go.

There came a time after five-years of a beautiful friendship - as lover, and working at a deep level with my teacher, that I fully owned being the teacher myself. Two alphas, that have their own soul path to follow. Many times, I was steered away from the Tantric community. I now understand why, as in that I maintained and kept building upon the potency, with no dilution. To allow the path to be revealed naturally, a path of soul remembrance, and the path of the shaman, into the darkness of the unknown. To keep leaping into the unknown, the beyond, and beyond the beyond. D is one of my best friends to this day as our love is infinite and free.

From this story you have read, there were many times over that my voice was silenced. Yet, it was 'I' who was keeping myself entrapped. The rest was an illusion within my mind and the stories I was telling myself. We try to change our past, to create a brighter reality.

> *"Until your heart is broken enough times, you will never know love, once your heart opens, love will never leave."*
>
> *– Rumi*

AN INNER VOICE OF WISDOM

There are three-parts that make up the soul. When our soul births in this physical body, there are three levels of Self. The conscious Self (our ego identity and inner child), the basic Self (subconscious mind and instinctive body wisdom), and our higher Self (guardian angel). It is our intuition that is the messages of the soul. Intuition is a sense of knowing, without knowing how you know, you simply just know. There are four ways to tuning into this intuitive wisdom - clairsentience (clear feeling), claircognizance (clear knowing), clairaudience (clear hearing), and clairvoyance (clear seeing).

We spend a lifetime learning to unravel and hear the messages. I have dedicated my book 'Completeness – A Doorway to Love', to the journey of our ego identity and that too of the inner child. This is a vital journey to explore, and I have touched on some facets here, though it is all interrelated and requires cross-referencing. If you have not read it yet, then make it a read, as you will gain more depth to this journey within. The messages of the body, inner knowing, and instinct will develop with awareness, patience, and practice.

Some may never trust in the messages of the higher Self. We are multi-layered, multi-dimensional beings, and this Life is a journey. There are three ways that I gather information to guide my life, and clairvoyance is the one yet to awaken. I feel this coming soon, if it is to benefit this soul mission, and the beautiful souls that I work with.

The soul speaks, and for many they are afraid to listen, always keeping busy, so it can be tricky to hear the right messages. It may take years to honour its truth and to have the courage to listen and follow through to be the light within the dark, a guiding spark of inspiration. It kept me sane to pretend I was going on an adventure each time I stepped inside those walls of the hospital. In the final 7 years of my career, each time I stepped into that world I felt my soul shrink inside.

In my spare time, I would do my inner work to come back to Self. I would write at night, to stay focused on my vision. I needed to be kicked out in order to leap fearlessly and leave my 23-year career. The lessons in life are there for our growth and evolution. I am sure you are beginning to see this. Here I was presented with another opportunity to break-free from the mundane and follow the heart-soul calling.

It was exactly to a day that it began, in 2016. I was suspended from my Nursing, because of complaints from patients. The funny part is, I didn't want to go to work, I was really tired, and my body needed to rest. I was fearful that if I cancelled my shift, they would take the shifts away from the Easter holidays. I was looking to pocket $2500. I was existing in a space of unconscious fear and lack. Lack of trust and faith in Self, God, and The Universe.

I was taught a lesson of lack. I ignored my intuition, went to work and attracted the perfect patients. Not one, but a collective. Our voices were unheard, I tasted powerlessness, worthlessness and hopelessness. The only thing to do when I was told the next day I was suspended until further notice, was to surrender. I did not surrender straight away, I went into a verbal rampage of complaints, that fell on deaf ears and brought more crap I had to deal with.

I realised I was dispensable, replaceable to them. It was a job. A casual Nurse has no voice, minimal rights. I was still not ready to leap. It was my fear, that created the perfect scenario. I had no idea how I would pay our rent, I trusted we would be divinely supported, a flight had been booked to follow my heart, to a soul in Canada. I let go even more and shifted disappointment into gaining a beautiful soul and experience of a lifetime. More of my inner voice became known.

I changed after the trip, owned my voice, to become clearer on my soul calling and sensuality path. Mum took the children and I on holiday, we were fed, nourished and loved. Following formal meetings and owning moments of unconsciousness, I was able to return on probation. One complaint and I was out. It was like walking on eggshells, and it was time to go there do my job and do everything I could to prepare for our future. I was learning to master silence, and work on the shadow interference.

A year later would bring more patients to complain. The interesting part is, all three- were of the personality stuck in blame. I saw how the system is run on blame, litigation, guilt and shame. There is an unwillingness to take responsibility for behaviour, what was created in their bodies, and the unconsciousness that many are living within; stuck in fear and anger. My attitude was that I did not want to be there, so I created the perfect scenario.

I find it interesting as the process would see others jump on the bandwagon. Complaints never voiced from six and eight months prior started to also be thrown in my face. I laughed what else do you do? It cut, yes, I cried.

Letting go can be scary, this had been a large part of my life.

My last shift, I was got covered in human faeces while cleaning up a patient and got it all over my shoes. The first time ever in 23-years, covered in poop! I removed my uniform, shoes, everything and placed it in the bin. Others were shocked, I was unable to say I was leaving, from signing documents to maintain my silence of the details. The agreement to go away quietly! And that I did.

I felt free, uncertain, trusting and began to free fall into the unknown. That was April 2017, and it is the most exhilarating ride, that has so much more to unveil. No regrets as my soul is finally free.

- Can you relate?
- Do you fear the unknown?
- Are you just existing?
- Do you honour the messages?
- Do you believe you will be supported?
- Do you have faith in the unknown?
- What does your life mean, and what is your purpose?

Our spiritual journey is to know thy Self, and to leap into the unknown fearlessly, with faith and trust. Faith and trust are your angel wings, and shifting the 3rd to 4th dimensions as Your brave Soul leads the way.

No matter where you are at, begin to make space for quiet time as there is power within stillness and silence. You cannot hear Your inner voice through the busyness and noise. A walk-in nature is a simple way to break-free from the chaotic day.

We must create space to allow intuition to come in. Nature is the doorway to increase our ability to hear intuition. Learn to trust in the messages and have gratitude even when you do not yet understand why it is happening. The bigger picture, soul knows, and this takes a willingness to trust in higher guidance. It is getting trapped in the ego body and inner child that will block the messages from being acted upon. This keeps the individual in a state of reaction, fight or flight, or feeling like the world is against them.

When you are in it, you cannot see it, as all rationality goes out the window

"There is a world within you with all the answers you seek. Beyond the external chaos." – Charles F Haanel

CHAPTER 3: THE HUMAN EXPERIENCE

> *"The cause must be mental, so in the mind, the mind is the creative force of what happens in the reality."*
>
> – Wallace D. Wattles

CREATIVE FORCES OF THE MIND

Some of you may have come across Wallace Wattles books or are familiar with this quote or have read it now for the first time on your path of learning. This is vital in seeing the big picture and to awaken an expanded level of understanding within the playing field of your life, and the universal collective consciousness. The teachings of great minds and thinkers such as Wattles and Charles F Haanel have inspired my Soul growth. Their powerful words have reminded Me of the inner wisdom that has always been within, the part of the roadmap in coming home to the powerful Self.

Here are a few paragraphs from The Master Key system, by Charles F Haanel. This has been a bible of truth for me, as my learning never ends, and I go deeper down the rabbit hole of awakening.

> *"Have you wondered how some people seem to attract success, the relationship, power, wealth with little conscious effort while others have great difficulty, others fail all together to their ambitions, desires and full potential?"*
>
> – Charles F Haanel

LAW OF ABUNDANCE

The power of creative forces is wonderful and magical. When there is diligence with correct application infused with concentration, then those blessed can obtain the desired results in their life. The Law of Attraction and abundance starts from the mental creative forces in the mind. The power comes from within.

The outer world will attempt to dis-empower and create a shadow of doubt. When one can adopt a confident and dominant attitude to take responsibility for their own thoughts, they can start to work miracles. Therefore, being mindful to who you listen to, is key. Therefore, the disciplined practice of meditation is key to daily living, and a way to breaking free of the mind.

Think of it this way, we have three worlds, an inner, an outer world and the meaning we create as reality. The inner world is filled with thoughts, emotions, and beliefs. The outer world is filled with experiences, circumstances and events that happen. The outer world acts as a reflection of the inner world. This will differ for each of us, depending upon individual perception, attitude, simply the way we choose to see/view the world. The only way to change the outer world, is to go within.

Hence why the stillness in meditation is a doorway into the inner realm of darkness. The spiritual path is walked, explored behind the scenes, and not a fake picture on social media giving the impression of spiritual practice. All self-practice is the unseen and all within the stillness of being. To then learn how to navigate this state of being present, into the experience of living, this is the true meaning of yoga - the art of living while being present.

The mind will and can create negativity. For generations, it has been handed down from our well-meaning and loving parents, seduced by the indoctrination of mainstream media and school system. These systems have capitalised on people's pain and suffering, feeding us lies, manipulating their power-positions, that have all lead to creating states of limiting thoughts and fears.

The mind will go towards whatever the individual is consistently thinking about. This will be at the conscious and subconscious level, visualising every kind of lack, limitation or discord. We create these conditions 'unconsciously' all the time.

This is powerful for teenagers to be aware of so that they do not integrate these false thoughts their lives.

To understand the Laws of Abundance, we must remember that the mind is the creator and the only creator there is. The mind is a lousy boss, yet a faithful servant.

Everything is mind, Mind is everything.

We are magnetic beings living in a physical body having a human experience, our emotions are creating an underlying magnetic high or magnetically low frequency. Some are all changing and vibrating at different frequencies, so we will each attract different things into our lives, no matter what we are each putting out.

WORDS AS S-WORDS

We always must rewind, to what we are consistently putting out. Our thoughts are so powerful, it may come as a thought, an intuition/ message or did you have some doubt and then you created the outcome. The thought may be thought very loosely with no real attachment, like a passing cloud in the sky, and then boom, it becomes manifested in form. The neuroplasticity of the brain can be re-wired, reset and new neural pathways created. I am proof of that along with many others like me.

It is the intention behind the word, the thought, the emotion felt while speaking the word and also the vibration that the word takes on in motion. Words are powerful and yet it is the feeling behind them that is even more powerful. It's like positivity, which is a surface level of feeling good, a state that is temporary, it will come and go, for deep transformation happens at a cellular level with conscious awareness of incompetence.

THE HUMAN EXPERIENCE

Many are walking around unconsciously spewing their toxic words, unaware that by complaining they are also slowing the process of what is trying to come to them.

When you listen to the complaints and join in, they are drawing you in to their drama/ you are choosing to get sucked in! Next thing, you notice the exact flavour of things start to show up in your life. Welcome to the mudslide in action.

You start off slow and before you know it you too are covered in the same stuff as your mate, feeling swept up, choking and drowning in shit! Some like to wallow in the mud together and many will be afraid to step out of it as it may mean walking by yourself for a while, alone. Until you find your vibe and your tribe finds you. Maybe right now, you have found your tribe? Or you may be looking to upgrade?

For many years I was learning to unravel the art of complaining and to fearlessly learn to walk my own path. Know and trust that as you step away from the outgrown relationships you begin to attract different people. It is a gradual transition for many, and for some it may feel like losing everything, in order to find everything.

There will be those you are drawn to without knowing why, where their energy is bright and being in their presence is uplifting. Then you step away, get caught up in your old life, the story, the flavours of drama and pathetic excuses and you feel drained, all over again. Your energy is depleted from staying in a situation that no longer serves you or is aligned for your greatest growth. Those around you feeding off one another, siphoning one another's energy, a chain of pain and survival. Trust me on this, when you are in it, you will not see it for what it is. Have souls in your corner that will back you up and show you the truth, and then have gratitude and loving kindness for those you step away from.

There is no judgement, only choices and free will.

There may be those that save you from failing into painful contrast of life, so you never fully grow into the powerful you. This may be blocking your success, having the rescuer always in the corner and playing the victim well, as it is an unconscious pattern. Over time this will knock your self-worth and is a form of unconscious manipulation, meet the wounded healer. Learn to rise empowered, be inspired to fall and be your change. There is no right or wrong, this is Your journey called life, your destiny is not going anywhere, and this isn't a race.

Listen to those that have their life together, walk their talk, and if you are fortunate for them to take the time to give you valuable feedback to what may be blocking your own success, then listen to them, even if it means biting your tongue.

Discern in all Choices

Be aware to whom you give your energy, unless it is a child. Never turn away from showing a child affection. Learn to hug, touch, and love a child unconditionally, as you too are honouring the reflection of your own inner child. Walk away though if you are angry and lashing out in rage, step away so your child is safe. Even the adult in reaction is coming from the wounded inner child, so maybe see them as a child and watch how your state of awareness shifts.

You have a choice to listen with compassion, or to not entertain what is being said, then walk away calmly. Life is about learning how to set boundaries, and children learn by what they see in the state of presence we are able to hold. This can be challenging when you are a naturally empathetic and suck up other's energies. It takes conscious awareness of learning to navigate what you take on (energy-wise) and what to allow to pass by. Using being an 'empath' as an excuse for heightened sensitivity is a lame excuse! It is simply an opportunity to honour the blessing you have been gifted, the ability to sense and feel deeply to the world around you. Learn how to protect, manage your boundaries and own your inner state. Living consciously during and following any interaction presented.

Yes, this will create a temporary separateness for them, yet they will never shift if you are carrying the load and doing it for them. It is simply how you choose to see it, your glasses and your perception and attitude to what is, it is hard to see it when you are in it.

No matter what, or when you step away, it all comes back to you.

Even the story that many unaware souls walk around with, the big bag that gets heavier and heavier. *"Hey beautiful soul, when is now a good time to put the bag down?"*

We have created it all, from our thoughts, emotions and attitudes to the meaning we gave circumstances, people and the events in the past. It does not exist in the now. The ego will not want to hear this and the individual will have no rational idea what is happening, and all they will see from a narrowed view is:

- Why does all the bad stuff happen to me?
- You don't understand, my life is so bad?
- You think you know it all?
- Even hurling the words; like 'Fuck you, you think you have your shit together all the time!'

It is a dance and the best thing to do when another is in full spin of reaction, is to hang up the phone, step away, walk away and create the space. This is a powerful opportunity of reflection to observe what just happened. With no complaining or talking about it, time alone is honoured to taste the reflection, and the ego is in full rampage of reaction. It can be scary to watch, even sickening and takes courage to see it all with love, honesty and self-forgiveness. This is how humility is learnt, within the dirt, and within silence.

Have the courage and willingness to be seen and maybe it is time to start to unravel, to step towards living a life of freedom pain-free and happy. Imagine what that would look like, smell and taste like and how will it feel?

- Do the work and you will all graduate.
- Self-love and self-discipline to work on you.
- The journey never ends, isn't this fun?
- We are all in this together.
- And we shall all rise in love.

The only world we can create starts with the inner world, that is then reflected as our reality within our outer world. So, it is time to step up and be the change you wish to see in the world. Be the leader you came to be and share those gifts with the world.

The Body Talks

Pain is a great messenger, whether the origin is emotional, spiritual, physical or mental. Do you see from my old story shared how I was unconsciously manifesting illness, disease and attracting accidents because of my thinking and attitude towards life? It is easier to look at another's life than to turn the mirror onto oneself. It takes courage to peel back the layers with love and compassion and a willingness to see the truth. The body will respond to the mind, where logic takes over clouding the view of the truth within the heart. It is learning to listen to intuition and breaking through the pain that gets created over time, as what awaits on the other side of pain is pleasure and freedom.

The body is talking to us all the time, yet many are too busy, numb or unaware/unconscious to 'feel' messages. It is only when the pain becomes so great and intense that humans listen and 'wake-up'. The challenge is hearing through and beyond the brain-fog of painkillers. Many souls are numbed out, checked-out daily with some drugs as drastic as horse tranquillisers. Welcome to the band-aid-mask of pain, and into the realm of games of manipulation of control. An example of unwillingness, unconsciousness and avoidance of taking personal responsibility. This numbing agent of drugs will never free the individual to shift whilst the mind is clouded with a toxic pharmaceutical fog.

The logical mind of reasoning, rightness and attachment to the old story adds to the illusion they are within. This aspect of mind will hide at all cost, projecting onto others and will be relentless until it wins.

It will deceive, lie, manipulate and blame everything outside of self, just to survive and get fed. The pain feels very real, yet is not the source of the pain, and the only way through is to remove the drug fog, dive into the pain with deep surrender, trust and faith in something far greater.

We are more powerful than we realise and giving power away to chronic pain is no longer an option. Once you have gained this awareness, to ignore it is ignorance. This is deep-rooted in fear. As it requires change, vulnerability and surrender of all control. The source is mental and has been created from deep feelings of:

- Hopelessness
- Helplessness
- Worthlessness

There may be resistance to forgive, or an unwillingness to walk alone and let go of the past. The past, the story of events will keep the individual trapped in their pain. Resistance to taking back inner power by staying stuck will serve a purpose by getting emotional needs met. These are met with attention, affection and acknowledgement of the story. The ego gets validated with the story, and to let go of the pain of identity, is death itself. This is massive to accept, and hence why many are stuck immobilised in the pain, and a vital truth to why it can take years to navigate this path.

To own this, takes courage and ruthless responsibility. To see the truth, requires gentleness, self-love, self-compassion and self-forgiveness. It is time to remove the victim suit, with kick-ass courage, trust and unconditional love. The logical mind will resist and tell you that you can't, as it wants to survive. It is being fed the illusion and lies, whilst answers await in the heart.

It is all choice, break free, or keep wearing it!?

While the lessons are being learned, similar scenarios will pop up into the current experience, with future experiences created. The same feelings of hopelessness, helplessness and worthlessness are tests to overcome with a new way of being.

It will feel very real like the whole world is out to get you, and that little voice of, "Why me?" It is not about perfection, as the path of the warrior gets messy. When you forgive, you set the attachment or emotional charge of the story free. This is not about forgiving the person to their face; it is about letting them go with unconditional love and to see a new way of seeing. This upgraded choice shifts the inner vibration and as the other veils of the illusion are lifted another piece of the unique soul path revealed.

Until life lessons are addressed, and forgiveness honoured, then the vicious circle can continue. Each time gaining more momentum, emotional charge and a massive reset waiting to present.

A traumatic event, personal injury, or loss that forces the individual to stop, pause or/and hit rock bottom in overwhelm and despair. This is a great opportunity towards deep inner personal transformation.

Contrast is sweet, to begin to see an opportunity presents to realign the direction of the path. Life may have to bring you to your knees in total surrender and humility to literally 'wake-the-feck-up and see the truth.'

The path least travelled is not the easy one, yet it leads to inner freedom. Inner change is ugly and uncomfortable, if it were easy and smelling of roses then more people would have their shit sorted out! And frankly, no shit that has been left to fester in the tubes will smell of roses, it smells breaking rancid! All shit smells off. End of story.

When you choose to fine-tune your energetic body and reset the system you will become more present, magnetic and attractive as an energetic and sensual being. The more the individual de-clutters and lets old stories go, crystal clarity and radiance is revealed. Souls are drawn to this resonance; they feel it and there will be many other energies approaching you.

As high vibration beings are drawn to the uplifting vibe of happiness, joy, and self-love, other beings, and entities will be drawn to a lower vibrational tone to feed off. I feel, see and read energy forms, within the physical realms and the magic of the unseen.

It is key to learn to interpret energy beyond the words spoken, and upon the path as an energy-healer-facilitator. It is wonderful to see through the lens of illusion to what you are being shown, and see each soul with unconditional love, forgiveness and compassion.

Pain will push back and hide at all cost; what is being shown is not the source of the pain. Tread wisely and always get permission from the individual unless you wish to get covered in their shitty mess.

A soul in pain, is not who they are at their essence, only the projection of who they think they must be, in order to feel loved, honoured and held.

We each have a choice to expand our hearts and know when to retract them to protect our energetic fields from outside attacks. Until everyone has worked through their pain body and taken daily responsibility to manage their own energy, it is difficult to grasp this concept. When you are in the position of the 'victim', this may seem backwards and frankly, mean.

Trust, as it is a path to freedom.

There are those who will unconsciously take, and those that will freely give energy with possibly giving in a way to get something back in return. Then there is a beautiful synchronicity of mutual energetic exchange in harmony with one another, that has free will and nothing to gain back and all to surrender into the ocean of oneness, this is pure unconditional love. The feelings will differ in the body, when they are mutual, there is an ease, openness and expansiveness.

When another is taking, you start feeling drained, a tightness in the throat and often too the solar plexus, the heart starts to feel closed, in order to protect. This may be as simple as retracting the energy, a setting of boundaries with non-communication, especially if you do not personally know them or are offering your services with an exchange of money.

There is no right, wrong or simple way. Life is about exploring experiences and navigating your unique path, even whilst finding the way out of the labyrinth of pain. All is free will and choice, and each layer of pain reveals a lesson and golden key to your divine mission.

Learn how to master your own energy and be wise in the choices you make.

CHAPTER 4: WHO ARE YOU?

"The Meaning of life is to find your gift. The purpose of life is to give it away."

– Pablo Picasso

A SQUARE PEG

We each are unique with specific gifts, either already known to us, or ready to awaken. Part of our journey is to learn how to evoke and access our gifts. I realised this was a vital key of the adventure back to my Soul truth. Once you know your spiritual blueprint/DNA, your life will begin to make more sense. There are many ways than this to access the spiritual blueprint. On the 1st January 2019, I was introduced to another way of revealing my unique blueprint and human design. Life will reveal the pieces of the puzzle when you ask, like the curiosity of a child.

What I am about to show you is an insight into the natural gifts revealed and the inner genius within. Throughout this colourful journey I created many different personas to try to blend in, and fit in, that over time left me feeling unfulfilled, and lost from a spiritual perspective. Feeling like I fit in nowhere, to suddenly people wanting to come and touch me as the freak in the room. This is me, the square peg in a round hole. This was insane, as it was soon revealed I was the *freaky genius*, suddenly people wanted to touch or connect with me.

It was weird to be on the receiving end as I had been the weird one, that did not fit in, was unheard and seen for my weirdness! It was time to start to see myself in a vastly different light, and honour what I had experienced; the journey of adversity started to make sense; there was a method to the madness.

These are the gifts of the heart and soul; your gifts are like fingerprints, or your spiritual blueprint/DNA. Your gifts are why you are here, connecting you with your essence, and with the rest of humanity in a deep and meaningful way. Another way of expressing your gift as a spiritual being in a physical body, is that operating from your giftedness opens you to receive the treasures of both the heaven and earth.

Whatever earthly things you desire are attainable with ease and grace when you are operating from a state of giftedness. In sharing your gift, it is natural with pure intention to serve and universe yields to your command. Knowing and working through the shadows unveils the gifts and ignites our superpowers (Siddhis). These are vital to your Soul mission, full human potential and activating your dream life.

The degree of ease and grace to create that which you desire, is directly proportionate to how you have refined and purified your intentions, so that you are coming from a place of authentic giftedness. Any incongruence with your truth will impact theses manifestations.

We get what we think about most of the time, Oops, that pesky little rascal that keeps thinking about all the unwanted things. Universe does not know the difference between good or bad - it simply hears what you think about, most of the time.

Once you wake-up and see the illusion (Maya) you are creating, there is no more hiding the truth. I saw other people's gifts before I was able to see my own, and to then have them shown to me, was one of the greatest treasures ever. To be seen, acknowledged and honoured by another epic human being, was beautiful. Thank you, beautiful soul, Shaune Clarke. That day shifted my perspective and you saw the magic that was unveiling.

I was told to explore my gift of expressing sexuality and I resisted it at the time.

I had to be ready and be doing it for all the right reasons and ensuring that all wounds were totally transformed.

Sadly, there are many expressing gifts from the wounded standpoint which brings more harm that healing, I see this much in the spiritual and Tantric community. This transference of unhealed wounds is unhealthy and manipulative in nature. Sacred sensuality is next level, so will leave that door ajar for another book.

We all sit within an intricate web of life and the YOU-niverse is within each of us. It is up to you to shine and allow others the space to shine too, as we each explore this adventure called Life! Even if you are unaware of your giftedness, it does not make you less valuable, it has no relevance, as each soul is priceless. Everyone has a place and all the time is an opportunity of coming into soul alignment, each uniquely poised and positioned. No one is going to take your unique place in the world! The more you chase it, the more it will elude you.

BREAKING FREE

There is a reason you are here and there in no one else like you.

Once you awaken there is no going back, as you are doing your soul a disservice by not honouring and expressing your gifts with the world. You may shift into a bigger arena and what you were doing drop away, the lessons learnt. You will attract the perfect teachers to facilitate your inner growth to unleash your giftedness. Look back at your own life story and have loving kindness of it all. You will have had doors slammed in your face with many 'No!' - all to propel you upon the perfect trajectory of your Soul mission.

Your gifts must be expressed for You to experience soul nourishment. By not expressing them, can and may lead to addictions, and other ways to numb out from life, a far cry from living free. It is the key to your health and resonance, and humanity is ready.

Every day that I get to access and express my natural gifts, my energy abounds. It is uplifting to be around and each breath dances with an inner power that is not over-run by the ego. The ego is vital to our ability to learn how to survive in the world, and as adults can be a rascal at times.

It is the inner work on Self that over time dissolves the ego, it is a fine balance and dance. Unless you have awareness of the ego and the power that it has over you, then it will continually create an internal battlefield of annihilation and seduction. The unravelling is a maze within a maze, and the truth revealed from the deepest chasms of the infinite heart.

There are no better gifts than your own unique gift set! To wish for another one is the ego judging what others have. We each have a unique place within the weave of the web/matrix of life, no one more special than the other.

I was suffocating my soul from the outside in and had to embark upon a journey to heal, from the inside out.

A FREAKY GENIUS

This is my unique 'freaky-genius' gift set. Most are on there so will aim to guide you to which gifts are your primary, secondary and complementary. Know that nothing is set in stone, these are playful guides, and watch how the ego pops up.

These are the results from the test I took. This is not an accurate assessment to base your results on, as you are not going through the exact questions to arrive at the answers to reveal your blueprint. You are simply reviewing the results presented. See what resonates with you, as you read through each one, if it feels good with your cells buzzing, saying Yes! then that is possibly one of your unique gifts. We usual have 1 - 2 Primary, 3 - 5 Secondary, and some Complementary Gifts.

Primary

Extraordinary Trust

Encouragement

Giving

Evangelism

Leadership

Beautification

Teaching

Wisdom

Mercy

Secondary

Hospitality

Cultural integration

Music

Knowledge

Writing

Facilitating

Complementary

Systematisation

Service

The only two gifts I did not have are Helping and Caring.

I believe 'helping' creates powerlessness for the person being helped. The helper feels powerful subconsciously. They feel needed, and this can become a trap for the child who goes through much. The wounded child and the wounded caring mother can both get stuck within this cycle of helping and being helped.

> *"Help children to do it themselves"*
>
> – Maria Montessori

'Caring' what others think creates the internal critic and people pleaser character. Over time, you stop listening to your inner wisdom by constantly caring about others and forgetting to put yourself into the mix. Learn to care about your own feelings and keep your nose out of another person's business. Care, but not that much.

'Mercy' is rare.

The gift of mercy is what The Dali Lama, Mother Theresa and Gandhi each have had.

PRIMARY GIFTS

There are strengths and distorted versions of expressions of gifts. I encourage you to check-in and see what resonates on a deep level. The funny part is, there may be one that you are 'Hell-No! that's not me'. This may be a key gift that you are stuck within the wounded or distorted version, commonly termed 'the shadow self'.

Encouragement

The ability to hold space for others to reach for their highest potential and more. These people are telling others how great they are and encouraging them to believe in themselves.

The 'wounded' believes in others more than believing in Self. A hurdle of limiting self-beliefs to step over, to see and start to believe in your own greatness. Build others up, puts self-down!

Does this resonate with you?

Giving

Is expressed through sharing uplifting and inspiring words, honouring other's physical gifts, acts of service with a generosity of spirit, a physical expression of generosity in pure form. They have a generous nature and giving nourishes their sou. So, when you receive their kind uplifting words, you are being lifted and feel it deeply within, with no strings attached.

Giving to receive and left feeling disappointed, leading to manipulating and attempting to control others. Giving the best head-job or sexual deed so he will never look at and desire any other woman. You see the entrapment?

Do you find yourself playing this out?

Evangelism

The ability to get people fired up about a cause, with a deep belief in the message. The message has so much passion behind it, you could shout it from the rooftops. This gift is used to manipulate others to do what they want, at the expense of other people, whether in business or the bedroom.

This is big in sales: to hook their target market, they tell you their story, through which they talk to your pain. This is the truth behind all marketing, they hook you in, then catch you.

Do you get passionate about something and must tell the whole world about it?

Leadership

Expressed through presence, some lead by example, some from the heart, and the evangelist leads through charismatic personality and compelling words. This person takes on the role of authority and you will feel their energetic presence when they enter a room, others will follow their lead. This gift is most easily recognised and is the purest form of serving others with dedication and selflessness. Leaders are great energetic givers.

Some try to attain it by overpowering and manipulating, due to their misunderstanding and distortion of the gift. To manipulate others to serve their own needs at the expense of others. We have all been on the receiving end of these and this is seen much in the personal development playground. There can be many games of manipulation and dis-empowerment going on, where one thinks 'I need you!' So, anyone who tells you they're not using NLP (neuro-linguistic programming) are telling sneaky lies, all to hook you in.

Are you a natural leader, or do you need to feel needed?

Beautification

The ability to appreciate beauty in ways that brings an object or experience from the realms of the ordinary to the extraordinary. This gift creates shifts in perceptions and actions. To embrace perceived imperfections, to learn that beauty happens from within. Choosing clothes that complement your own unique style, or a love for make-up. Great at inspiring others into action whether from the boardroom to the bedroom.

Inability to see own beauty. Manipulating others by the make-up, breasts and seductive clothes enticing others in a web of seduction to get needs met.

How does the gift of beautification resonate?

Teaching

The ability to impart information and knowledge to others in a way that the information is easily understood, and the lessons remembered.

Getting stuck in the head and becoming disconnected with your truth and inspiration to teach others. This can happen in the schooling system where a teacher's natural gift to teach is impeded by jumping through many hoops to stick with the curriculum; their giftedness and passion gets suppressed and suffocated. Obsessed with shovelling and forcing the information down the students' throat, the playfulness and sparkle lost.

Have you experienced this as the student or as a teacher, be honest? How can you shift this?

Wisdom

This individual had gained a vast resource of wisdom stored inside them. This may have been collected over years and from a higher wisdom that they can tap into. They see and sense knowledge that exists within and without, in a field of collective consciousness. They see patterns of events and draw insights from them with effortless ease. There is an innate knowing and intuitive insight from the realm of the sub-conscious and super/higher consciousness from within. They could sense and SEE the bigger picture. Without the gift of wisdom, humanity would be much slower in growth and evolution. Change makers see the vision and the reason why we are here, they simply know and need no reassurance.

The wounded will use their wisdom to manipulate others with information. In the game of the ego, there is a fine line and it is vital to remember to have humility. It can be easy to be seduced by the ego, thinking the 'wise' are more advanced and more valuable than others. It can bite you on the ass when you least expect it.

To come to wisdom, it takes these three things:

- Wise discernment
- Humility
- Forgiveness

Are you downplaying your brightness to make others more comfortable? Do you put your partner down unconsciously?

Mercy

A constant state of empathy, unlike the gift of encouragement, where you can achieve an unusual capacity of empathy. With this gift empathy never switches off and is a constant. It can be draining to be around people too much, so taking time out alone is a must, to nurture the inner light with ways to feel good. Apparently only 20% of people have this gift with the ability to move on, leaving details in the past. This has been a saving grace in the journey of relationships and lessons in love. To seek freedom and deep understanding, within the darkness of the unknown. The wounded takes advantage of others in their time of need, seeking approval to feel needed.

Do you see yourself with the gift of mercy?

To forgive everyone, see no evil, see no bad, and love all no matter what they have done to you?

SECONDARY GIFTS

<u>Hospitality</u>

Expressed predominantly through acts of service it can also be expressed through presence. Others that are receiving will feel deeply cared for, about, and even deeply loved. This is valuable in a coaching setting, to create a safe space so clients can open, feel secure and nurtured. Vital in the intricate web of life, it gives others the feeling of being loved with no attachments or expectations.

To give, in order to meet their need at the expense of others is a distorted expression of this attribute. For example, giving a massage and then expecting one in return, giving with a sense of reciprocity, or obligation in others in order to manipulate or control others.

How many of you have also done this, or something similar?

<u>Music</u>

Expressed through composing or playing music, singing, dancing or simply having a great appreciation for music. Music reaches deep into the soul and has been used throughout history to impart knowledge and infuse individual and collective consciousness. Music is one of the most powerful forms of storytelling, with the ability to shift consciousness.

When a person uses this gift to manipulate others to serve their own needs. For example, think of the groupie following the rock star or band, where they become revered and often idolised. This creates an inflated "self-importance" meeting the musician's egotistical needs and desires. They may also use it to manipulate others by writing music and lyrics to influence the thoughts and actions of others in a selfserving way! Think of politics, mass media, popular culture and war propaganda that use music and lyrics to manipulate people's perceptions, thoughts and action.

How do you feel when you hear and/or play music? The body and soul never lie.

Knowledge

Encompassing of a broad range of topics, it can be applied and conceptual knowledge of inner wisdom. Always gathering and have insatiable curiosity to know and learn things. They may never feel full of knowledge, as there is always more to learn; they love to read books and listen to accelerate their growth. They may throughout their lifetime amass incredible depths of knowledge on many varied topics. This assists in creating new levels of awareness, to assist others in expanding their minds with individual and collective consciousness. This sweet synthesised gift helps others stretch their minds to new horizons and beyond. The great minds have studied information once held by the elite class, now open to people like you and me.

The internet has allowed more freedom of knowledge-gathering, which is exciting for humanity. There is a movement of 'power to the people and awakened evolution.' The powers in authority positions uses this on others.

If someone has gathered a new level of insight and awareness, then are withholding the information, there becomes a distortion. The banning of books, the withholding of knowledge and even the elite class, going right back to the time of the Egyptians. The other way is when the insight and knowledge is gained, and they do nothing about it, hiding as they have a fear of failing. This is another definition of stupidity and fear of their greatness.

Are you holding back your full potential? What is your unique story to share?

Do you share knowledge openly and are you sharing what you know with your children?

Cultural Integration

An insatiable interest in other cultures and feel no distinction that creates separateness between yourself and people from other cultures. Travelling will feel easy and you have an ability of being able to adjust very easily into the flow of the country; you will be intrigued, fascinated and inspired with the contrasts of culture. With this gift one has an insatiable curiosity about people and places that create different cultures to the ones they grew up in.

People with this gift are great business people as they are great at building relationships, and really understand life and have great clarity. Their communication is open and honest with a genuine interest in others. They facilitate greater connection with humanity and provide a channel for the wisdom of families, cultures and societies outside of those environments. An ability to build trust easily one may use the gift to get something that they want at the expense of another person or manipulate others to get what they want.

Do you love to travel and experience different cultures and do you build relationships with others easily, no matter their cultural differences? Facilitating The ability to hold the space for an individual or a group of people that moves them in the direction to reach a common goal with a strong presence. They have the ability to make the process more fluid, smooth and far more efficient and will respond in ways that neutralise strong and negative resistance. They have great influence over others!

People with this gift have an ability to read body language, the energy of a room and act accordingly in the moment. They have their own opinions yet have a gift to see another point of view and communicate this, so they feel seen and heard. They are exceptional listeners, skilled observers gaining more insight into situations and scenarios, so working towards sustainability and working together cooperatively in order to bring balance to the planet. This is vital as the world moves through so many big shifts. Some happening right now as those with this gift will ensure a smooth transition from one way of life to another, that is necessary for the future our beautiful planet.

Used to manipulate someone or a group to reach certain outcomes or goals that serves a personal interest at the expense of others. This is used in clever marketing, where you are led to believe you are all one, yet it is mostly one person benefiting at the top. Facilitators are smooth, great talkers and you will be unaware that you have been caught in the slipstream of the trap. All 'methods' are traps. Yet you need the methods to discipline the inner work, to awaken the guru map from within, to eventually free all methods and be free.

Do you notice when you are present and in your heart? Does this resonate? And why?

Writing

The ability to write and express in a way that will move people to affecting their thoughts and perceptions, with a positive impact on them pushing action into perpetual motion. Anyone who can write words that influence people's thoughts, perceptions, emotions and behaviour has the gift of writing. There is a writer and a soul story within each of you. Your voice is unique!!

Everywhere we look, clever marketing draws on your emotions to manipulate your decision to buy because you think you need it. It is the way words are twisted by a clever reporter, to make the story juicier and more appealing. It is the gossip in the magazines, which are a distraction from tapping into your inner wisdom; it dumbs you down and distracts you from living. The food companies that put "sugarfree" on the packaging and then add in toxic sweeteners. Everywhere you look, there are hooks that feed on fear!

Choose wisely who you listen to, and what you read. Do your own research.

COMPLEMENTARY GIFTS

Systematisation

People that take the visionary leader's idea and bring it into physical reality. They have a great ability to manifest as they clearly see the big picture. They have strength to bring creative inspiration into tangible reality, by breaking it down into bite size pieces and systems. This gift is vital to the service and value to the world. In a world of chaos and conflict, they can bring sense and order to life to inspire others to do the same.

An inability to cope with the chaos and attempt to control everything; they become very ridged in their ideas and must categorise everything, so they feel more in control. They can become lazy, arrogant and get complacent in a place of authority and power and may miss the big picture; they are caught up in the categories of the system and create drama.

Is this you? How are you when you are not expressing your gift?

Service

Similar to the gift of giving, gift of helping and the gift of hospitality. These are all enabling gifts and assist others in feeling valuable and cared for. This inspires others to step up into their full potentiality and live their life with restored purpose.

Someone who provides a service that enables, yet also harms others. For example, countries building weapons of mass destruction, and the pharmaceutical industry.

Do you share this gift? Wake up to those that are using this in a distorted way.

Chapter 5: What is Blocking You?

> *"You are one thing only. You are a Divine Being. An all-powerful Creator. You are a deity in jeans and a t-shirt, and within you dwells the infinite wisdom of the ages and the sacred creative force of All that is, will be and ever was".*
>
> – Anthon St. Maarten

Unlocking Your Greatness?

No matter where you are at, you can begin to love all of you. No matter if you are emotionally shut down and numb on the inside have faith that you can shift. It is time to start showing you how to tap into a magical and mystical ability, and a journey towards embracing the beautiful and sensually powerful you. This will prepare you for the next book in the series. Your Soul chose the body you are in and made the best choice for what you are here to learn and to begin falling in love with you again.

It is time for embracing the Divine body you have and honour every aspect as beautiful. A path to sensual awakening is owning your power, to love, nourish, express your sensual tastes and to never feel shame again. To release the bondage restraints of judgement on the deep and mysterious hidden passions. It is time to break free of the illusion and lies that you have been fed and brought up on. This is about having the most delicious relationship with yourself first, a beautiful journey to personal power. It is time to own your greatness and light others up around. We are all equal and learning to be human, that means being humane to all beings.

The biggest turn off for a man is hearing the complaints of what a woman thinks is wrong with her body. This behaviour draws attention, so he starts thinking that there is something wrong with it.

There is something about yourself that you do not know. Something that you will deny even exists until it is too late to do anything about it. It's the only reason you get up in the morning. The only reason you suffer a shitty boss, the tears, the blood, the sweat, and it is because you want people to know how good, attractive, generous, funny, wild, and clever you are.

"Fear or revere me, but please think I'm special. We share an addiction. We are approval junkies. We are all in it for the slap on the back and the gold watch, the hip, hip, hoo-fucking-hoorah. Look at the clever boy or girl with the badge, polishing their trophy. Shine-on, your crazy diamond, because, we are just monkeys wrapped in suits, begging for the approval of others. If we knew this, we would not do this. Someone is hiding it from us, and if you had a second chance you would ask why?"

This is the commentary of Jake from the movie Revolver, played by Jason Statham, where he addresses how the ego is completely concerned with the specialness and its need for external approval. The ego will bring much internal suffering, where it is in discontent and is on a path of searching for incessant approval from others. It is funny we are taught to feel special and then we must learn to let go of the specialness as it is who we think we are! The illusion of the ego!

> *"The greatest enemy will hide in the last place you would ever look."*
>
> *– Julius Caesar 75 BCE*

Is it the clothes we wear, the different fashion trends we explore, the friends that stand out, the colour of our hair? All to get noticed. With many breaking free of the mainstream and going to the other extreme, making a statement in a vastly different way. All to get noticed! The focus is external (outside of ourselves), so it is up for judgement and approval from others, are we good enough, do we fit in, are we accepted. The pain goes on.

The problem is that we have become so focused on the physical that we have lost sight of where beauty comes from. It is hard to escape it, we are addicted to approval, bombarded with the media, fashion magazines and the social media giving us the up-to-date trends of the rich and famous. This external stuff we are led to believe that if we have the latest fashion accessory, we will be happy and complete. It is so shallow, yet many of us get caught up in the clever marketing and the inevitable brainwashing. It is everywhere on social media platforms.

The marketing is clever, it is to seduce you into buying their product, it is what there number one role is. It gets us every time, we think we need it, it will make us look sexier, more attractive and without it our life will be more difficult. They play on the emotions, as that is where they know they will get you hooked.

Foods that will dumb you down, switch off your insight and inner wisdom, sedate your inner joy and happiness and keep you coming back for more, seduced and into the game of addiction. The distractions you see in the shiny magazines, the rich and famous, and the mindless gossip are all decoys to the truth. Once you see it and with awareness you awaken, you can make a conscious choice not to entertain it. Observing it is like watching a movie, the masses being controlled and allured into believing what they are told.

Welcome to the Matrix!

THE ENEMY WILL HIDE

Images of the rich and famous promoting their newest plastic surgeries and latest trends are used to lure you, and leave you feeling inadequate and unhappy. Better still, see the hidden truth and the insecurities of these people in the limelight. It is up to the people like you and I to ensure that a healthy message is getting through to you, your children and their children.

Love the skin you are in; your perceived imperfections may be another's admiration of your unique perfection. Stand proud and embrace it all, even the things you think you have done wrong, yes dissolve the sin and guilt you keep yourself trapped in.

WHAT IS BLOCKING YOU?

We have forgotten that our perceived imperfections can be our greatest gifts, we were born perfect for who we are. Many of us have had to learn to grow into our skin, to embrace the differences, and move past the physical. The physical is impermanent and will change with time, no matter how much we try to slow down the process.

We have forgotten to embrace the real beauty and have been hooked into comparing ourselves to others. In this competitive game, all leads to inevitable suffering and blocking the view to our happiness, and creative success.

Your greatest enemy is the Ego, Your internal critic.

> *"Only something as vast and deep as your real self can make you truly and lastingly happy."*
>
> *— Nasargadatta Maharaj*

Our self-esteem is core to learning to love and embrace our unique beauty within. When self-esteem is in depletion mode, we look outside seeking approval, and this is where the ego can play tricks on us. The ego creates fear to hide behind, ultimately it is fear of being found out. Fear is an illusion within the mind, fear of not being good enough, not fitting in and fear of rejection.

Many will avoid it at all cost.

It may be a belief formed as a child, leading to feelings of rejection and abandonment. Do we really see what is in front of us or is the perception clouded and tainted? We want to fit in to what we are fed by the media, our social group to feel accepted and acknowledged; society is starving for attention.

I invite you to pause and feel into your core and answer the following list of questions. Allow the first things that come up and jot them down without hesitation. It may be a random word so do not over-think it by analysing, simply get it out. The logical mind often blocks the truth from being revealed and expressed.

- What has reading about my story brought up for you?
- What sensations did you feel and where in the body?
- What can you learn from what came up?
- How did it feel to consider your own story/background?
- Is there anything you do not want to own from your background/past?
- Write it down, this is for your eyes only, so put the judgement on one side.

Judgement will come up; it does not just disappear overnight. See it, acknowledge that it is there, and put it on one side.

- What did you dislike about your past?
- Do you feel any shame?
- Are you angry?
- Do you blame anyone for your past?
- Do you feel drawn to the past, going over old stories?
- Do you find it hard to forgive, and let go?

- Have you lost trust in others/self?
- Do you know what you desire?
- Do you know who you are?

Did you answer Yes to any?

Be honest, for until you can be faced with the most important person that exists, you will never shift. You are the most important person in Your life, and the only story of lies, shame and blame You keep feeding, is Yourself.

We are our biggest critic. It is our greatest hurdle and it is about learning how to get the way of ourselves. The time is now to make room for the new and improved beautiful, sexy, sassy, classy, goddess or god that you are.

BREAKING THE CHAINS

See emotions as an inner guidance system. There will be those that are out of alignment, and those that feel in alignment with their core beliefs. The out of alignment will feel off, while the in alignment will feel good. When they come up see what your beliefs are and if you need to change your perception to what you are seeing. It is when you can start to change your perception to what is, that you start to create a new way of seeing and experiencing. Gradually you will start to live more in alignment with your specific core beliefs. It is time to start feeling more and become less distracted by what the eyes see. The view or movie playing out will be predetermined by past experiences, current attitude and perception. It is vital to change and upgrade the old programs that are running your life. In order to grow we must work on Self, to become 'Free' of heavy density and embark upon unravelling through our own self-created spirals, traversing towards the Sacred heart.

By the 5th dimensional realm there is no right or wrong, no good or bad, and there are multiple realities within the present moment, it is infinite love for all. This is where each soul begins to choose the reality they wish to experience. And until the lessons are learned with upgraded ways of being then the same patterns will continue. Humanity is shifting through the density of the 3rd to the sacred heart of the 4th dimension. This is very apparent from my story and will relate to many, as you begin to see the patterns in your own life. Therefore, sharing this has been so powerful; I hide nothing and am shameless.

A belief is a thought that you keep thinking and we can each change a belief anytime we choose. Many beliefs people live by are learned from the environment in which they were raised by well-meaning parents or caregivers. I say well-meaning, as each soul can only be to the extent that they are aware of, in that present moment. Old beliefs formed in childhood may be out of alignment with inner soul truth, then the environment may be the perfect catalyst of experiencing contrast within the souls' journey. A belief can be the greatest lie you feed yourself every day to avoid feeling into the emotions.

These old beliefs may continue into adulthood creating an internal dysfunction keeping the soul stuck in chains, and that may also be part of the path chosen before choosing to experience this lifetime. It takes responsibility and ownership to shift beliefs, to begin living with conscious awareness and consistency tuning and checking in within present time reality. Within your current reality, there are simultaneously parallel realities of choice and we can learn how to shift into another of which we desire. The only one getting in the way of You living the life You desire is

WHAT IS BLOCKING YOU?

You, and a weak strength of will! It is time to get off your ass, stop bitching about your past, stop complaining about what you see and shift your inner state of being. It is time to move, now!

Try this exercise:

Firstly, release the physical and jump up and down and shake your body. Open your mouth and as you exhale, say HAAAAAAA.... that is right make a funny noise as you exhale, if anything it will make you laugh, which is good. You may even want to scream, yell and shout. All is welcome, there is no judgement, after-all it is simply stuck stagnant old energy. Do this for 2 minutes, jumping up and down on the spot!

Next, stand or it still, softly close your eyes.

Feel into your body - it will be buzzing and alive.

Exhale everything, empty your lungs, so there is nothing left

Even make a big juicy sigh, let it all out.

Take a big inhale through the nose, fill up your lungs

Pause at the top

Big exhale open mouth

With a big yummy "ahhhhhhhhhh sound"

Repeat 3 times

Then sit quietly, eyes softly shut, lips slightly closed, focus on breathing in through the nostrils and out of the mouth.

Tip: focus more on breathing out, the inhale will automatically happen for you. Sit quietly and just focus on the breath, when the mind wanders as it may, come back to your breath. Enquire into the emotions and see what old belief can be upgraded into alignment with your current truth. Know and trust that everything is healing, and everything is okay. Notice where you feel the emotions.

Time for a 'Higher wisdom' check in.

When you ask your highest self a question, and you think of a person or scenario, the answer will be felt within the body. To allow the answers to follow, there needs to be stillness and quiet. This is not about thinking with the right brain, the logical side, this is about allowing the answer to reveal as a feeling or sensation within the body. As a meditation practice gains consistency then concentration and ability to focus will sharpen. Questions are to be direct with a Yes or No response. This is different for everyone, some may hear words, see images or experience sensation, and with practice these will strengthen.

INTUITIVE MESSAGES

This is about learning to listen and trust the intuitive messages, vehicles to access super-powers, of clear hearing (clairaudience), clear seeing (clairvoyance) clear feeling (clairsentience), and clear knowing (claircognisance).

Trust your intuition and messages of the soul, logic and force cannot be used. This is explored in greater depth within the final book of the series, 'Soul Codes – Remembering Your Mission.'

WHAT IS BLOCKING YOU?

- 'No': A tightness in the throat to the heart - constrictive, restrictive, heavy and choking, or hearing no. I hear the word loud; some see a stop sign. It is all different for each soul. You may also hear an UGH-UGH and may feel nausea.
- 'Yes': In the Solar plexus and heart - expansive, light, full and free, and hearing yes. You may receive a tingling message in part of the body, this is different for everyone. I also get a yes in my sacral area with a rocking and a AH-HA.
- 'I Don't Know': the sound of UMMMMMMMM. Pause until you get a response of either Yes or No. Play with some other inner questions and then come back to it.

Intuition does not tell you what you want to hear; it tells you what you need to hear - the messages have always brought me inner peace of knowing. The more you trust, listen and act on the answers, then the more you strengthen these gifts.

Thinking of the person will also be felt within the body. When you are thinking of them and it is out of alignment then it will feel restrictive and tight, or you may also be out of alignment with your Heart truth. When checking in, this may be a message that you are not expressing your own truth out of fear of rejection, experienced as throat tightness, and coughing – a direct message from the throat chakra (energy centre.) It may mean feeling uncomfortable by unintentionally hurting another, by saying 'No!', and they experience rejection.

Think of a scenario - a fantasy and be guided by what your body is telling you, or a direction your soul wishes to explore, experience and express. The judgemental mind has a pesky habit of getting in the way of free expression and awakening the spirit! How many men or women are pleasing their partner and not expressing their deepest desires? Many have lost their voice, afraid to be heard, or express their raw truth with confidence, fearless of how it may be received by another.

- How would it feel to say what you desire, and open up more?
- Does your partner support your journey/is it time to explore your path?
- Do you know what you want?
- How would it feel to say No?

We all make choices, and choices create consequences. The consequences being the Life lessons. I used to think it was 'karma', yet there is neither good nor bad, simply lessons of cause and effect. Once you start to gain more awareness, and connect with the body, then each soul will naturally become more attuned to their truth. It is time to honour your truth and break free of the old armour of protection.

All the inner wisdom and answers lie within you.

WHAT IS BLOCKING YOU?

<u>No Excuses</u>

If money was unlimited

What would you be?

Your scars dissolved

Infused, a fresh possibility.

What would you be?

Imagine a state

Free from the judgement

Free from hate

And self-created insanity

A distorted reality

Bullshit excuses

Who is the muse?

Imagine being five or six

Unlimited imagination

Not giving a shit

No longer a hostage of

Your mind's bullshit

A victim of your circumstances

BREAKING FREE

Who cares?

Stop blaming, cursing and

Fuck that shaming.

Start to dream a bit

And keep building your vision

Everyday commit to grow

Come apart in tears

Make getting up your mission,

Repeat and never give up! Be inspired

To follow your bliss

Ducking and weaving

Others' fucked up bullshit.

Your choices and dreams

Your newfound reality

Be the change No more excuses

You are love and light

As the only real fight is always within.

WHAT IS BLOCKING YOU?

Work on your vibe
Then find your tribe
People that inspire you
To love you
And guide you
Never to catch doo-doo again.

To hold you accountable
So, you can grow within
To reveal your divinity
Raw authenticity
Rare Beauty blossoming
And never to be
Hidden within.

Being Free in our Spirits, 1970s

WHAT IS BLOCKING YOU?

Being Free in my Spirit, Sedona 2018

Chapter 6: Freedom from Shame

> *"You do not need to seek freedom in a different land, for it exists with your own body, heart, mind, and soul*
>
> – BKS Iyengar

Feeling Trapped

Your mindset has been crafted by what has happened to You in the past. Boom, truth-bomb, reminder, the story is keeping you hostage! The inability to let go of the past, your perception to it clouding the view, and lessons passing by, not getting taught with an inability to move on. It is time to stop feeding the insanity between your ears by carrying around the past as a cloak of wounds. It has served you well, but it is time to put it down. A mask to hide the unworthiness deep within, the mask to gain attention of the pain eating you inside, so be courageous and put it down. I have a gift; it is magical and bright and is a new coat to wear with love. It is the 'coat of honour 'and will assist each Soul who chooses to put it on. To access strength, ignite an inner bravery and have willingness to do the dirty work upon the earth. Most vital of all, 'Never give up!" again. What you have experienced is here to be transmuted into your gifts and service for humanity, as being the light of hope and inspiration.

Each day we each have an opportunity to lift someone up. How about lifting yourself up first, each magical day. To meet your reflection with a smile, a gesture of love, gratitude, appreciation and being that change of lightness in your world.

Imagine if everyone on the planet was doing this daily and impacting their local communities. The world will never change, until each soul is the change itself.

Are you ready for change? Are you getting in the way of the self-sabotage and an old program of negative self-talk? Why do we react? And are you getting high jacked moment to moment?

The body takes over in reaction mode, and our wiring set for a pathway. This has been a stress response learned over time and it is also for our survival as a species. If we learned it, we could also unlearn and rewire it. Yes, you can re-write the story.

The Fight-or-Flight Response

Danger – Panic-fear, reptilian brain kicks in with a release of adrenaline into nervous system and the sympathetic nervous system kicks.

Survival Instinct – Sustained reaction of fight or flight response: running, fighting or freezing in action.

Surrender – Tears with acceptance of nothing left to give.

Insight – Clarity and awareness, reflective insight of what just happened.

Action – Ah-ha moment, an opportunity to create a new way of being from the insights; action replaces reaction. New patterns of behaviour begin to be rewired.

How many of us have found ourselves at all phases, with your boss, partner or children? Getting stuck at 'Survival Instinct' is scary and brings up feelings of being out-of-control, with the inner-negative talk in rampage. Here is why I shared this with you.

For many years I lived in the 'Danger' and 'Survival Instinct' phases with moments of 'Surrender'. As a result, my body went into lockdown from my throat to my pelvic floor. I was living in reaction-mode on hyper-alert the whole time, was exhausting.

This impacted my body at a physical, social, psychological, emotional and spiritual level. This may relate to how you feel, feeling like you are walking on eggshells, scared of 'what if', and the smallest of noises makes you jump. Be gentle as you 'inquire' within. This has served you well in protection. I can still feel it kick in at times, that pesky programming runs deep, and yet with awareness you can begin to break-free of it. This is the state that I witness, has become the social norm for many teenagers.

Where do you consistently live?

Be brutally honest as it is easy to skim past this bit, as the mind and voice in the head will not want to be found out. See it all with gentleness and kindness.

"What we are seeing out there is the projection of where we're at - the projection of the clinging of our minds."

– Ram Dass

Within each body is a potent nectar and sea of fluid that is constantly moving within and around our energy field, a life-force ever present, all-knowing and ready to serve us with our deepest desires. When our life-force stops to flow, it is then that we are officially dead, no longer within our body. You see, the fact that we are energy means that we cannot die as we simply change form from physical back into ether/space/consciousness which is omnipotent. It is everywhere and within all spaces within and without, an infinite space of nothingness. Absorb this a little, especially if you have never heard of this concept before.

'The breath is the anchor to becoming present in the here and now, it is the one thing we can learn to control, as well as the mind. The quality of our breath and how we are breathing will have a direct impact on our health, wealth, sexual desire, manifestation, success and all the things that happen to us in our lives."

– Einstein

We can go weeks without food, days without water, minutes without oxygen, but not even a nanosecond without our Life-Force. I have learned some rare few can go months without water and food. Remember we are energetic beings, our energy within a physical container, we need movement to assist the flow of water within the body; the breath creates the magnetic flow within the current - the positive and negative. I will keep it simple, so you can start to get your head around it. It is our breath, which moves this Life Force within and through every cell and tissue of our beautiful body.

Movement is as vital as the ability to relax and be still within the present moment; it's a beautiful dance and balance within the flow of life.

Our breath is key.

Breath is the doorway to presence.

Learning presence is a game-changer in all your relationships, and most importantly the empowered You. Get ready to connect deeply with your body, mind and soul. Presence is a learned behaviour, anyone and everyone can attain it. The bottom line is many are unwilling or unconscious to do the inner daily work. The inside work that happens in solitude, and then brought into the game of life in the playing field of reality, to the test if you are ready to shift to the next lesson in the experience of being human. That is the beauty of being in the best school ever: Galactic School, a fun progression on from Earth School.

ENERGY AND ATTENTION

Having negative feelings toward attractiveness can have a negative impact on sexual desire, and the health of your body. These distortions may have come from your early caretakers (parents or carers). It may have stemmed from a parent who was constantly obsessing about their body and as the child listening, absorbed the negative self-talk like a sponge. It may be from criticism, from a boyfriend or girlfriend or from kids at school. All these influences can have the potential to undermine your sexual self-esteem, to the point where you feel unlovable, creating a distorted view of the world. This imprints upon the psyche and the belief system created and may transition into the need to please others with an inability to say 'No!' Feeling drawn to sleep with many different partners in order to feel an experience of love with surface level beauty and attractiveness validated. On the inside, it feels empty, and a void that searches to fill up never feeling satisfied.

The biggest turn off for a man is hearing a woman complaining about her body.

The complaints, the perceived imperfections, the put downs, the nasty remarks, they all hurt you and damage the beautiful and sacredness of your relationship. It is killing the passion, and how can he or she really love you when you are putting yourself down. It is a turn off and it is time to stop this destructive habit. Being a woman, it is also a turn off hearing a man complaining about his body. Your body is always listening to you, every cell within your body vibrates with the frequency that you are feeling, so choose feeling good thoughts. Talking mean and angry things will create an environment of low vibration, which will attract more low vibration things your way. The same goes for blame, shame and guilt, they will create low vibration energies and waves, an acidic environment, ideal for cancer, disease and viruses to take hold and affect. Let us reveal these pesky hidden tones that craft many souls' daily reality.

- Shame
- Blame
- Guilt

As mentioned earlier there is a correlation between STDs, illness and the active vibration within the individual. When you can shift and elevate the internal vibration of the individual then the virus can no longer live there; it will be eliminated from the body!! Again, take what you need from this, this is not about persuading you. Follow your own inner truth and become curious. This may have been created by an imbalance of essential mineral salts in the body as it has been attempting to come back into balance.

BREAKOUT TO BREAKTHROUGH

The journey from the early teenage years, like many, these were the hidden feelings of my inner world:

- Self-loathing
- Hate of my body
- Disgust
- Guilt
- Shame

- Sadness
- Resentment
- Anger

Living from a place of hopelessness, helplessness, unworthiness, and unhappiness, I had created a limiting belief as a teenager thought 'If I ever have that, I would rather be dead'. WOW, that is a big fat-ass belief!

When I found out about the Giardiasis (a parasite, that causes diarrhoea) I also discovered a sore on my labia. My heart sank, overcome with fear. Fearing the worst, I made an appointment to see a doctor, who gave me the news.

"You have Herpes Type 2 and it is the worst one you can have and you're forty, you've had your kids and had your fun. Now you will have to modify all your relationships. You will never be able to have sex without a condom and you will not be able to have a normal sex life, again".

These were his exact words. What-the-fuck! Wow talk about having zero compassion.

Me: (Defiantly, choking back the tears) 'I will find a cure, there has to be one!'

Doctor: "No, this is incurable, you have it for life."

He made it sound like a death sentence!

The rest was a blur. I drove home in shock, tears streaming down my face, met with the intuitive voice of angelic wisdom, 'Do not listen, you will find a cure.' I knew, believed and trusted this was part of my journey and that I would find a way to eliminate it for good.

Firstly, I had to do 5 things

- Take ownership
- Be accountable
- Take responsibility
- Wake the fuck up
- Be badass with my boundaries.

Always have open disclosure to those that may be at risk once you find out! This was to be a pathway of inner freedom from guilt, shame and lies, and expressing my voice. What I learnt was that there is freedom in this, and I was met with nothing, but love, humility and compassion. The light of self-love began to shine. This was to become an integral piece within my inner healing to love myself deeply again, which started with taking full responsibility for my life. The thing I most feared, I had to learn to love and then let go of.

I refused the suppressant therapy and searched the Internet. What I found made so much sense. It is amazing as still society attaches shame to it, especially the medical system. Their responses made me feel helpless, hopeless and fed my feeling of lack and unworthiness and feeling my life was over. It was starting to become noticeably clear that I had to heal on the inside. There was much soul healing and self-love to accept and start to recreate a new way of living. I stayed away from doctors as they were coming from fear and helplessness. My family, I told I would find a cure; they were devastated with the news of me having it. What I was learning was that both the parasite and the virus hides out in the gut. Wow, it started to make sense.

I was searching for a detox to eliminate the parasite too and that is when I came across a New Zealand company. They had been trialling one of their developments and the at the time, and the testimonials of subjects felt truthful. I felt a new wave of faith and excitement, like every cell within my being was saying 'Yes, do it!' The soul knows, so I leapt in faith and put trust in the unknown.

I ordered the detox and began the journey. My family were sceptical and asked about the research. I understand they had concern for my well-being, as I was heading fearlessly into the dark and they had witnessed this in the past, as many times I fell flat on my face.

They also are from a medical background where everything is backed up with approved medical research and clinical trials. I was doing it anyway. My response was expressed with conviction of ownership. 'The testimonials resonate and what do I have to lose?' I believed in it with my entire being and rewound back to my limiting belief.

Belief is powerful, I see this in everything. Unless you believe in something it will never work, as 'Belief' is a thought which creates a positive vibration. I once heard a doctor say, it is never about the treatment, it is always about the patient and if they believe in the treatment. This is one of the truest statements ever. I felt like it was Christmas, a precious gift to give me my life back, I was on my way to healing, like a brave knight going into battle, I entered the battlefield.

FREEDOM FROM SHAME

It was time to kick ass lovingly, and the first three days I was shivering hot and cold, like I had a bad case of the flu. The virus started to be drawn out of my body, and I had initial panic kick-in and the question, 'fuck am I dying?' I reached out to the company via email and felt supported. I dived deep into my meditation practice, changed the water to high vibration alkalised and ionised Kangen water - the best antioxidant for the body I was aware of at the time. I began to shift the vibration of circumstances, and emotions with focus on inner work engaging in yoga, meditation, raw foods, Resolve Detox, and hibernating to heal and self-love.

After three months there was a massive energy shift in the way I was vibrating. My body felt different, clearer and energised. A dark cloud with shadow of fear and shame had lifted, and this felt good. The outbreaks stopped and I felt renewed and restored.

The active vibration was emanating at a higher frequency and my focus was on feeling good. During that time, I began to gaze admiringly at my yoni/vagina in the mirror, every morning. A wildflower love session of self-love and appreciation to her blossoming yoni-uniqueness. This led to embracing and loving all aspects of my body at deeper level and further explored in *Wildflower- Reclaiming a Sacred Place*.

I fully embrace a bush; this is next level of feminine freedom. I also now love beards on men. Hail the full bush woman and bearded man.

It is true for energy, where energy & attention goes, so energy flows.

For years I had been sending angry thoughts of shame, blame and resentment to my beautiful yoni/vagina/pussy, so I attracted the teachers who would mistreat, dis-empower, and hurt me. I attracted the unwanted STDs as I felt so much shame of who I thought I was.

The journey perfect for healing and I believe a massive breakthrough in medicine with the power of the mind, thoughts, emotions and how the body will reflect what is happening at a cellular level. It is time to love ourselves deeply and accept our beautiful bodies, as we are all YOUnique. I am blessed to have experienced this and to understand the contrast and the power of our mind. We can cure anything, and everything! This is my belief. On a cellular level, some of the medical industry will not want you to know this, which is crazy when it will help so many people across the world.

The majority (80% of population) have some strain of the herpes virus, so who is judging now?

Is that you?

When I say this, who is judging, and where is the judge hiding?

PAY IT FORWARD

I stand here proud to share this very vulnerable part of my story, I have no shame, as I have healed my mind and body. To be free of this pesky rascal for eight years, and still be clear. This is empowering, never again will I hide, it is now time to make some noise. Years after I had done the treatment, I recall listening to Kevin Trudeau on his Radio show talking about the cleanse and found out he is an advocate for the detox. He, and many others have simply done the cleanse, since 80% are carriers and it is a great mineral detox, he is a man who is an advocate for being a messenger of the truth. I was excited, as my gut is always right and spot on. He went on to say that anyone that gets pimples on their back and but, shingles, cold sores are all strains of the herpes virus.

Having said that, you can always get re-infected from another who has the active virus. Imagine if everyone acted and had a clean-up with this detox?

The government will not want you to know about this, they will hide the results at all cost as the truth will set others, like you and me and someone you know, free. This will piss off the Pharmaceutical industry, as they will have to convince buyers of their drugs by making the global population believe it will make then healthy and free from Dis-ease. If you know anyone with this, then pay it forward as there is no need to suffer in silence or ever feel shame again!

Not allowed to call them cures, there are remedies for ulcerative colitis, rheumatoid arthritis, HIV, HPV (human papilloma virus), Hepatitis B and C. Why aren't individuals allowed to say cure; go figure? Go with what feels right in your gut and never think of giving up faith, and trust that there is a way to rid this from your body and have a very normal sexual relationship virus-free.

Some doctors and society at large make having Herpes sound like a death sentence when there is a way to eliminate it. I believed growing up it was a death sentence from the stories I had heard at school. Society thrives off dis-empowerment, hopelessness, fear and helplessness. No wonder disease and sickness is on the rise.

Suppressant medication rather than addressing the root cause is a band-aid. Think about it, we are treating the 'symptom' and not the root cause.

Be mindful of your thoughts and e-motions.

Start to love you,

Love your yoni,

Love your lingam

Make resolve with your fears

Use mineral detox!

Be very mindful what you are focusing on, and then be grateful for what life brings as it is a key to your journey back to you. More have been coming forward who had been silently feeling alone and ashamed. From a simple openness to share this information, giving support and love, has already created a positive impact; let the snowball of change continue.

Let me ask you this? Would you tell everyone that you have had Glandular fever or Shingles every time you start a new relationship?

I guess not!

Safe sex is a great bet, until you know you are choosing to be exclusive with one another. Observe their nervous system and the consistent frequency in their energy field of being. Be shameless with your choices and I invite you to do a detox.

Make your own conclusion on this, from what you have already been shown into my story of what I had to go through, to overcome and heal on a deep level, this will show you that anything and everything is possible. It is vital to learn how to read another's energy as a man with an unconscious penis, or who lives a negative life will be penetrating you with a toxic low vibration wand. The same goes for a woman that is living a toxic life of complaining, and has a depressed unconscious vagina, it will be an ocean of negativity in there and it will feel uninviting and cold. I am not making this up, it really can be felt once you are awakened and energy sensitive.

This is not to bring more shame, this is to begin to be the change and raise your awareness of living a conscious life in happiness, joy and freedom. Be mindful who you invite in and share in intimate offerings.

We can all learn to be free together!

It is time to stop creating more of the shame and lies you are fed by the media, and some within the health industry; start to take back your power and step into the powerful You and heal your inner world, own life and body. In life if you are pointing the finger in judgement, there may be a few lessons in store for you to come - just saying! Attention and focus are powerful.

An Awakened Perspective

See through the manipulation

Within corporation and Constitution.

A freedom of choice

All twisted and tainted Dissolution and pollution

A possible misuse

An old paradigm

Labels attached

That aim to dis-empower.

Take back your power

Have freedom of choice

See through the lies

No longer imprisoned with fear

Take back your rights

Honour your truth

A choice of responsibility

Reliability for self

Take ownership

Invite humility

Personal accountability.

FREEDOM FROM SHAME

Be willing to see
You created it all
The disease another label
Your inner hell
Keeping you small
To love the bits, you hate
And explore deeper within.

See the bigger messages
Your power taken away
Possible abuse, manipulation
The places you shamed
The people unforgiving
Messages manifested now ready to be heard
The experience of hell
The fears keeping you stuck.
Unresolved emotions
Ready to embrace
Willing to be healed.
No more place for disgrace

BREAKING FREE

All created from anger

Possible misuse of power

Expressions of hate

Unresolved anger

Shame and blame

Keeping you stuck

Now living in pain

A fucked-up game!

Fall in love with every inch of the body

Especially your unique lingam, and yoni

The STD's expressions of hate

A new love beckons and awaits

The divine being meeting you at the gate

Perfectly beautiful

There's no mistake

No need to hide

To stand apart

No longer a victim

Self-love and acceptance

Never to leave you

Living forever free within your heart.

Chapter 7: The Naked Truth

"We all wear masks, and the time comes when we cannot remove them without removing some of our own skin."

– André Berthiaume

Peeling Back The Masks

This is great to explore by yourself or with a friend who is honest. Even better to explore with your partner. No judgement please, this is an opportunity to start being brutally honest. This is key to being able to grow and evolve within a conscious relationship.

'Revealing the masks' translates to:

- No more games
- No more hiding
- Time to peel back the layers
- Time to shine like a crazy diamond
- Your wild inner crazy released.
- To breaking free.

In Latin, the word origin 'persona' comes from mask. The persona being the role played by the actor and being referred to as the theatrical life. (Dictionary.com, LLC and Wikipedia).

We are all actors in this crazy game of life, and each mask is an aspect of our personality. No wonder so many have gotten trapped in the drama of the multiple masks they are wearing. For example, a Soul meeting a lover will wear a vastly different mask to the one they wear for their spouse.

WHY DO WE CREATE THE MASKS?

To create a different character, to hide the mask of truth, or to step into another role. This may stem from low self-esteem, not feeling worthy of or to simply hide what is going on at a deeper level. They may have been there to protect you as a child, teen or young adult, to stop feeling pain. Know that now is a safe opportunity to open into you as a beautiful and lovable soul, to love you deeply. I put all these together as I was feeling lack in all of them.

- Lack of pleasure
- Lack of love
- Lack of happiness
- Undeserving of love
- Lack of joy
- Lack of trust
- Lack of faith.

Your biggest hurdle may turn out to be your greatest lesson.

We are powerful creators that have forgotten who we are, and many of us are creating our worst daily nightmares.

Reasons why many have forgotten the powerful self:

- Hushed and told to be quiet as a child
- When speaking-others do not listen or hear our words
- When speaking, others finish of our sentences
- A different view on the world, trying to fit in
- Avoiding conflict at any cost
- A belief of not being good enough
- Getting angry is not acceptable behaviour
- A belief we are not worthy
- What we want does not matter
- A belief we are unimportant.

This all comes down to one thing – Love.

This brings us to our self-esteem and learning to become rationally selfish! Selfishness is self-preservation, and anyone with children will know this. Selfishness is loving yourself deeply, as you are worth it. If you never take time for you to grow, then what do you have to give back? This is even more vital when you are the only adult in the household. We can learn to create a new and improved belief, any time we choose.

A belief is just a thought that I keep thinking.

A belief is just a thought that I keep thinking.

A belief is just a thought that I keep thinking.

A belief can be the greatest LIE we feed ourselves.

> *"Behind every mask there is a face, and within that, a story."*
>
> – Marty Ruben

To hide fear, we create a mask. This protection and projection of survival serves a purpose while we are growing and needing to protect those areas of pain inside - emotional, spiritual, psychological and physical. It is stuck energy. Masks serve to protect, hide behind and create a facade so we are not seen or found out!

The ego will defend itself at all cost.

It also may be there to avoid other critics and judgement of who they think we are, and may represent that which we feel we are, at a soul level.

Who is now running your life and internal programming?

THE NAKED TRUTH

While you are wearing a mask, it will be hard to see. You will attract the perfect souls to embellish further ingraining it into your psyche. Part of your personality, the ego feels stroked with attention and affection, "Wow, that is a trip! "All with this running dialogue.

- It's not fair
- It's so hard
- It's exhausting
- Why does it always happen to me?
- The pain is too much
- I've tried everything
- Nothing works
- I can't do it anymore
- No one understands
- Why me?
- You will never understand how I feel.

This is draining your energy, giving your power away and creating more suffering in your future.

It all comes back to you.

This is also arrogance and specialness of being different than everyone else. Your mission is to clear up and work through your soul-life lessons as you are here for greatness. This is your inward path to awakening your soul purpose while removing the blocks within along the way.

If a friend, partner, or work colleague keeps dumping their shit on you unconsciously, know that you may be caught within their drama and destructive energetic field. It is essential to create safe boundaries.

- Step away when you can
- Set boundaries in the time you spend with them
- Do things to fill up on love
- Send them compassion
- Send them love and forgiveness
- Stop entertaining it, as it will suck your life force
- Trust and accept they may never shift
- Fill up on love and be love

Masks may have been created, as others were judgemental of your free expression of who you were discovering as a teenager and young adult. This also serves to protect the soul from being attacked. Some may get covered head to toe in tattoos to create a persona to put people off, or they may simply love the expression of tattoos. Others may hide behind the make-up. Whatever it is for you, allow it to serve you for as long as it needs to; when and if you are ready you will remove all masks and truly be seen. Some may work with dangerous people and so give a disguise for the identity to protect that who they adore and love. Some feel they still must hide behind a mask due to public opinion; I believe this must change, think escorts and prostitutes. They are no better or less. To judge is to judge Self!

We can play with masks and inter-change to gain deeper understanding of Self and others. Then we can be faceless, where we dissolve the mask all together.

As children we dress up, play, and explore different costumes. Even as adults when we dress up for parties, we start to take on the personification of that costume and character. It is fun, playful and can expand the creative imagination. Even dressing up for your partner for your bedroom fun!

Masks may serve to protect the innocence within our sacred truth that may have been abused, tainted and misused, and we are not ready to see the beauty. So, you see they each have their place in our human development, and over time inevitable transformation. They may protect the perception of others' judgement by the way we think we look while being distracted from our soul truth. They also provide a sexual allure of fantasy and deep curiosity. We want to see and unwrap what we cannot see behind the mask and underneath the costume.

> *"Oh, the allure of the mask and the unknowing of seeing someone's face, a fantasy created in the mind."*
>
> *– Zoe-Anna*

The illusion of the vision, and the revealing of their face may bring disappointment and shock, as you may have fallen in love with their mind and the words they expressed. This though, is far from truth and is hiding and not revealing the true self. Make sure you become the detective, check out everything you can about them especially if they are only showing you a small piece, and especially if they never show you their face. This may seem obvious and can easily escalate when passions are involved. This is a powerful message for youth and the intimate connection that can happen in a chat room. Ask who is behind the chat, and why are they not showing their face?

- Why are they hiding?
- Why are you hiding?

- What are you hiding?
- Are you ready to be seen for you?
- Are you ready to reveal the naked truth?

Many are not ready for the relationship as they are yet to honour the relationship with Self. The beauty in each relationship is teaching us lessons about Self. Even the abusive one presents hard and ugly truths, especially if it is a pattern of being unwilling to take self-responsibility and own your reality by stepping away. Many want to attain enlightenment yet are unwilling to put in the self-practice behind closed doors, to remove the layers, so they remain living in an illusion. Some are unwilling to get down on their knees and eat the dirt when they fall. That means putting in the inner messy work and to keep getting up, no matter what it takes.

Some may want the quick fix, unwilling to do the daily work; life will bring the perfect contrast. Others may be jealous of your success, and this gives them direct contrast of where they are at and where they wish to be. The most challenging of relationships is the one that does not catch your shit and never draws the line in the sand. If you are blessed to have or have experienced one of these, you are blessed. They see your potential and see your beauty and yet will not entertain and catch your 'bullshit' or language of lack. There is no hiding, no sugar coating the ugly truth and they may not be your best friend that you bitch, whine and complain to. By the way, if you are that friend who sits and listens to all the bullshit, you are being dumped on. You are allowing your energy vampire friend to feed off you. The masks can be deceiving and will hide at all cost. I recently learned to see another layer. A vampire has to be invited in, so be mindful who you invite to share space with. We each get to choose, as we are all learning. Bottom line, you create and shape your reality.

No more free feeds!

There comes a time in your life, to be free of all the masks. To allow others to see the true essence of You and for You to fully embrace and own it all. We can re-define the meaning we give our past. This is not about having your shit together; Hey, I am far from perfect, and the learning never ends. This does not mean that you must catch the crap either, as there comes a point that these people are also blocking your path.

There comes a time to step up, step away, own it, possibly fall apart and then rise from the ground up.

Wise discernment is an art to master, send love first, forgive and step away!

When meeting another or forming a connection that you are choosing to be intimate in, then this requires openness and no hiding! It is all about trust. Be aware of the person that you have not seen their face, heard their voice and the only interaction you have had is through writing and messages. There is no character in this, and soon you will start to see the cracks appearing. Thank them for the lesson and move on. It is our business to remove our own masks and not force another to remove theirs, all is free will and choice.

Faulty Wiring Patterns

I experienced many faulty wiring patterns as you may have seen from my story. I have unveiled many masks of the victim I played, as I mastered them all, shamelessly. The masks of the victim I dive into in my book 'Completeness – A Doorway to Love'. This is an invaluable life experience with brutal honesty and humility that will expose what you cannot see. What I wish you to take away is that breaking free is related to our ability to do three things:

- Take ownership
- Be accountable
- Take responsibility

This is the first step towards personal freedom.

This will also depend on four other things, and this information I recall hearing over and over in audio format, by a messenger that it now has become a part of my sub-consciousness and a new and awakened way of thinking.

Thank you, Kevin T, for all that you are being, and the truth you unleashed to those ready to listen, and willing to do the inner work.

- Who or what do you listen to?
- What is your willingness to learn?
- How teachable are you?
- Repeat the first three, every waking minute.

Your willingness to learn will depend upon your willingness to accept change. Having to change everything and everyone around you all the time is exhausting, the only thing you can change is You. Your attitude, emotional state and perception to what is, is what needs to change. How about starting your day differently; put on a different energy suit and go about your day and see the world through new eyes.

Let us now look at a Law of Facilitation. From a great friend that explains this Law so eloquently, a Soul I love and respect, Steven Michael Petersen.

> *"As neural impulses pass through a certain set of neurons to the exclusion of others, it will tend to take the same course on a future occasion, and each time it traverses this path, the resistance will be less. The nervous system will condition itself to find the path of least resistance. With conscious awareness of the new habit and new neural pathways will be created over time. This is also the basic law behind muscle memory. The nervous system requires time and spaced repetition to adapt to the upgrades so there is adaptability and mastery at each phase. You push the nervous system before it has time to adapt and 're-wire' and it can do the opposite, go into overload and shut down. It gets uncomfortable at times; this is part of the process and a new way of being."*
>
> – Steven M Petersen

This is the way that I re-wired my physical body over time (years) and is exactly why it is vital to deal with the nervous system with love and respect. We are habitual beings and can replace old habits with healthier and more harmonious ones. Begin today to play smart by creating new habits that serve humanity and Your own Spirit.

This index will determine how teachable you are:

Unconscious Incompetence – Unaware of incompetence

Conscious Incompetence – Awareness of incompetence

Conscious Competence – Awareness of competence

Unconscious Competence – Mastery of competence

This takes presence, persistence, discipline, determination, honesty, humility, self-forgiveness, and moment to moment ruthless application. Throughout life, you will move through this training balance scale, and every time you challenge yourself to grow and learn something new, you will start at the level of unconscious incompetence. Life will throw you a curve ball and you will get to learn the lessons again. The journey will be unique for whatever you are here to learn. There is no need to remain a victim of your circumstances or current situation. These inner challenges are perfectly aligned for what we need to learn, grow into, evolve, and rise above and beyond. This is about shifting through the layers of the illusion that we have been conditioned to believe.

Chapter 8: The Pink Elephant

> *"I learned that courage was not the absence of fear, but the triumph over it. The brave man is not he who does not feel afraid, but he who conquers that fear."*
>
> – Nelson Mandela

Fear Unpacked

Fear can be the best motivator, especially when you are the one that has to make it happen; flip the fear in drive and sky-rocket determination. Learn to mind your own business of the competition of others and focus on your own creative passions. Unless there is a lion or grizzly bear chasing you, fear is self-created and extremely destructive, when consistently active. Here are some common fears.

- Fear of conflict
- Fear of failure
- Fear of rejection
- Fear of the future
- Fear of speaking up
- Fear of not fitting in

- Fear of being alone
- Fear of other opinions
- Fear of love- giving and receiving
- Fear of your greatness
- Fear of commitment

This will be negatively impacting your life happiness and blocking you from living a life of sensual and sexual freedom. The freedom to allow your body to let go and be able to orgasm with ease and express fearlessly your thoughts and desires to your partner of choice.

From the story, I would fight, run and freeze. In relationships with men, any sign of conflict and resistance I would freeze. I did not start out this way initially, I would fight back then after much violence, I learned to run and hide.

DO YOU FIGHT?

On the back foot ready to fight, the one who loves confrontation, and creates drama to fight more. With feedback they go into defence mode, with their blood boiling in seconds. They are ready to pounce, taking what you say personally, reacting and defending what they have, in order to survive. When you find yourself in a relationship and you are both fighters, watch out and run for cover. Something needs to give, and the better fighter comes off the least hurt. Be the one that draws the line in the sand. Be the one to walk away in peace and stillness.

Do you run?

Any sign of confrontation, you run, hide and avoid confrontation like the plague. This is exhausting, as no matter how much you run, eventually you will drop in exhaustion. Something will happen to make you stop in your tracks and start to face that which is scaring you. In this state we run from drama to drama, stuck on the treadmill of fear. We can each learn to release and shift to re-wire the system over time. Life may force you to stop, by an accident, a trauma, an illness or a sickness.

Do you freeze?

This is immobilising and paralysing. It is highly toxic, as the dumping of the stress hormones gets left festering in the muscle tissue. When you curl up, you become frozen and cannot move.

You are like a sitting duck.

On the other hand, freezing, can also be a saviour, especially if you are a child in the line of fire. By hiding and freezing you may be away from the toxicity of the fight between the parents or care givers, or the abusive relationship. Out of sight, out of mind and in stillness. These souls will avoid confrontation, hide and say little.

Freeze can then go onto the inability to express what you need in any moment, from your parents and partner. In a relationship you may be unable to express what you like or need. You go into autopilot, as you fear confrontation and rejection. This becomes the people-pleaser who never feels deserving and worthy to have their desires and needs met. They fear rejection and deny their own feelings and desires.

Are you a fighter, runner or do you freeze?

The person You are with you have attracted, they are your teacher and You are theirs. The layers of the heart may take years to loosen. The heart will release when it is challenged to be vulnerable and ready to be brave and open. Nothing happens by sitting on the fence, no one will give you your life on a plate, you must be willing to play the game, or get played.

Within society there is another layer that is keeping souls trapped from expressing their raw truth, it is rage. Rage of what they have experienced in the past, rage of what they are unconsciously suppressing - shame and its darkness of denial, and rage towards others that have fully embraced their sensual essence. The sensual (r)evolution that we are living within, is happening and this is part of My Soul mission, to dissolve this distortion. Rage is creating a greater separation within the human psyche and is explored in greater depths within Book 2, Wildflower – Reclaiming a Sacred Place.

MOVING FORWARD

It takes conscious effort and discipline to keep checking in, this can feel brutal at the time, as you learn to let go with ease of what no longer serves your journey. Now is the time to put down the bullshit game of blame and shame for good. Stop blaming your kids for being late, for not doing what you want and step back out of the drama, which you are creating. With your friends, have those in your life that will pull you up in a heartbeat, for they see the truth beneath what you are showing them. It is not about letting go of the memories of the past, it is about transmuting them into your greatest awakening. Everything that we have experienced, are challenges to grow from. To go deeper within meditation and being willing to do the shadow work. Doing the shadow work will re-program the current reality with the ability to shift the past, by going into the memories.

This starts in the home. It is easier to live this way in the outside world, yet within our family homes and intimate relationships hold the buttons of reaction, keeping us hostage. Be gentle with this, believe me if does not happen overnight and we are all leaning and growing in this crazy ride called life. The colourful crap that came out my mouth, and patterns ingrained into my nervous system looked ugly. With awareness, persistence, patience and practice it will become easier and you will come out the other side. This will continue until the insight is gained. Be willing to see it all, as ugly as it may appear. Learn to love the imperfections in behaviour, see them with compassion and have less resistance toward them.

RE-CAP AND RUN DOWN

Stop blaming your partner for getting home late, especially when they are living with purpose. A man finds his happiness through his passion of purpose creation, it juices his soul, and every soul chooses freedom to be.

The people he wants to spend his time with are the ones he loves, his family. He will still be thinking of the next big idea when he is with those he loves. It never switched off. I understand this, it's the same for women who are living with passion and purpose. It is a magnetic energy when couples can work together and be the support one another needs. This is a gift and a magical journey with one another.

Stop blaming others for the mindless stuff of the house. Begin to see how much blame has become a normal part of living. It is also something that will change with time, awareness and conscious living.

If nothing else, take away this next golden piece of wisdom as the keys to 'Breaking Free' from anything that happens in your life. Refer to this simple checklist as you free the shackles that keep your restrained.

Ownership with Honesty

- Conscious awareness
- Honesty with humility
- Acknowledgement
- Be courageous
- Trust in it all working out
- Have faith
- Belief in you and those you love
- Daily inspired action
- Expressing your purpose with passion
- Share your gifts with the world
- Recognise & acknowledge your magnificence

You hold the Power to create the desired or undesired – you get to choose your life, it is time.

Accountability with Action

- Create a contract with you and you
- Hire me as your coach, there is no hiding
- Join a tribe of souls
- Keep a journal
- Create goals and take daily action
- When you say it, do it!

- Own your shit, moment to moment.
- Stop with over apologies of sorry
- learn and shift
- Empower your children to pull you up when you raise your voice
- Be kind to self, and others, as tripping up is part of the dance
- Keep getting up when you fall
- Empower your teenagers and stay calm in conflict with them.
- Catch the excuses and laugh it off, I see you.

Be accountable on the spot and follow through; baby steps first but keep taking more. In the moment with your children, teach them to be honest, humble and let us keep it raw and real.

Ruthless Responsibility

- Awareness
- Breaking the pattern
- Choosing upgraded words
- Speaking with conviction
- Follow through with positive action

Be the change within your family, relationship and circle of friends. Become the teacher of self and not the preacher. Lead by example, walk your talk empowering others to rise and do the same. Be You and stop trying to be like others. Yes, feel inspired, and then express it as yourself.

Be aware and know that there is no such thing as perfection. When children see parents and adults always being right, they start to feel not good enough wondering, 'how will I ever match up' and 'I am a bad person as mummy and daddy are always right'. Age is not a prerequisite for wisdom or awakening. Your children, teenagers may be wiser, and more enlightened than you. Teenagers have rapidly evolved consciously, by watching our falls, learning, growth from our souls unravelling. Teenagers have compassion and heartfelt gratitude that your parents have done most of the inner work for you, it was an aspect of the conscious wave they chose to play a part in. It is called conscious evolution of our species. To come into the potentiality of the Quantum field, where everything is instant, moment to moment.

Notice how small children naturally treat others with love, kindness and compassion and, possibly more than you right now. Give space so they learn to lead and keep empowering them to be their greatest versions of themselves.

Ownership, accountability and responsibility starts at home, and is the best place to begin with your own family tribe. They too have a vital life purpose to follow; our children are gifts on loan from the universe, so guide them well.

Never stop playing your unique game of life.

Conclusion

"The truth is like an onion; it has no effect on you until you start peeling away each layer."

– Zoe Bell

The end is always a new beginning, a fresh canvas, the start of exploring the unknown within, another exciting layer to unwrap. There are no results unless you are willing to peel away the layers. This peeling and undressing are protection of the ego. The sensitive layers are to be honoured with the highest level of self-respect, loving kindness, gratitude, forgiveness and compassion. Life is an infinite dance, a magical miracle moment to moment.

"The rawness is equally the richness, the painful reveals the pleasure, the resistance, a new offering. One cannot exist without the other, all aspects of the whole."

– Zoe-Anna

We are magnetic in nature and there will be those that repel and those that draw together. There will be souls who, when you meet them, it is like you have known then forever, and these are part of your soul family. In saying that we are all part of the same soul family, it is called Love. When a soul pushes, then is willing to soften to dissolve the fight and the charge, in truth the only fight is within you.

There will be souls you meet that flip your heart sideways and you both feel it. This magnetically charged energetic soul connection, aligned with your active vibration is a magical process. It may be for a moment, a week, a month, a year, time is limiting on something that is infinite in nature.

You may have an instant connection with another who is married and you both share the feeling of being lovers in another lifetime, even many lifetimes. It is refreshing to acknowledge this openly and respect one another's choices. Soul lovers' chemistry bends space and time, where two souls collide, and they meet in the dimension of Eternity. This is the inner work that I guide couples and non-partnered souls through, to access this portal of deep inner bliss. A connection of raw vulnerability with totality of presence. Once the inner 'phire' is ignited, they have the potential to access it, infinitely. We are here to learn from one another, and souls will magnetise to what they must grow and evolve from. Some soul lovers may leave as quickly as they showed up, so as best as you can, have no attachment to any of them.

Each relationship and interaction hold a message to unravel, and time has zero relevance on the depth of intimate connection experienced. To be free of attachment is the final intention of breaking free, as to hold on is to create inner suffering.

The question is: How deep are you willing to go, to discover what you do

CONCLUSION

not yet know? As you do not know, what you do not know.

Some souls may come in for a season of change in your life, the perfect catalyst to shift you from where you are at into the new and expanded version of you. Others for a lifetime.

CONCLUSION

Family members that you have resistance with are teaching you valuable lessons of what you need to understand or love on a deeper level. It maybe to also shoot rockets of desire into a totally opposing direction to beliefs that you grew up with. Everyone you meet is a reflection in some shape or form. The eyes will distort the truth and only see what the perception allows. This also holds for the ears, as they will only hear what they choose to hear, clouded and tainted by the perception and emotions playing out within the body at the time.

A deep soul connection is a feeling that stays whenever you think of the other person, which is most of the day, and night. They are in your dreams…

Your souls dance in the moonlight energies entwined.

Their resonance abounds within and without.

He or she is the last thing at night you think of and the first thought you awaken with.

Often waking with a smile, a laugh.

There will be those that are so like you it is like looking in the mirror.

Your soul family, the relationship is easy, effortless and you share a deep resonance of love.

Each exhale is an opportunity to let go, to lean into a new possibility of being. No matter what you have experienced, it does not define you. There is no comparison with adversity, it is real and raw to everyone. No better or worse. It simply is what it is.

Life is for living and shamelessly expressing Your Soul.

The more we hold something in, the less room we must remember Love. The more we cling to what was, place blame, shame and guilt, then the more we suffocate the soul. It is time to change the beat of the drum, to Your own rhythm, to stop punishing yourself, and to rise into your greatness.

Embrace each sacred moment, shift your perception and you will begin to see a new world of possibility. Breaking free is an individual choice, it begins and ends with self. If you are still confused or confronted, then I suggest you put this down for a while, and it will draw you back when you are ready.

Life will present the lessons of sweet invitation to open the heart's door. Everything is choice. It is not about having all your shit together, it is the willingness to be honest, courageously imperfect, and letting go of what no longer serves Your highest purpose.

Letting it go is a way to be free, and when you are ready, then it will be waiting your return. There is no force, and a pause maybe the perfect delay until you are ready, to gain the awareness and reveal the truth. Conscious living is about remembering your humaneness, learning to be more present, patient and gentle, as we are all in this together. We can never change the past, the fact is, it is no longer happening in this present moment. It is past, no longer active, and the only thing that is keeping it active, is the attention to it. To shift the attention is to gain awareness, and to gain awareness, is to evolve consciously.

Here are some summarised examples, from my story.

My dad left home, and my dad left home.

I was raped, and I was raped.

I was beaten up, and I was beaten up.

I left my marriage, and I left my marriage.

I killed a teenager, and I killed a teenager.

Abandonment and rejection are now being released and cleared from within and around me.

I am grateful for the family I was birthed into, the karmic lessons learnt around relationships with men. To transmute the victim games and unleash inner freedom. My Dad taught me to follow my heart, and that true love is unconditional, and forgiveness is freedom from the past. Feelings of unworthiness, self-hated of being raped are now being released and cleared from within and around me.

I never consciously chose to be raped; I do believe that I chose to experience this before coming back in this soul lifetime.

Co-dependency and violent acts of abuse in relationships, are now being released and cleared from within and around me. I never asked to be beaten up and accept my part in the game of co-dependency. I am grateful for the shadow of co-dependency, to awaken the gift of sensitivity and begin to understand the depth of sacrifice, and to follow My Soul mission.

Feelings of guilt and dishonesty in relationships, are now being released and cleared from within and around me. In expressing my truth, I liberated My Soul to Be Free. From learning to be intimate with my own Soul, I re-discovered Love. This has awakened the ability to be transparent in all relationships and Love all unconditionally.

Feelings of guilt and self-loathing of killing another Soul are now being released and cleared from within and around me. The road fatality was an accident, I forgive myself for something that was out of my control. I am loved, and I am whole.

I am worthy, I am complete, and all is love.

I take full responsibility for who I am being moment to moment. I get to choose a new possibility of being. I take full responsibility for getting drunk that night, fighting with my dad, getting in a car of strangers that I met in the bar. And all the events before the rape.

I take full responsibility for possibly being distracted with the radio that I never saw him on the road until it was too late. I take responsibility for fighting back like a wild animal, not honouring the beautiful women

CONCLUSION

within, and not stepping away sooner each time others were reaching out to assist me.

I take full responsibility for my actions and forgive myself for not honouring my intuition earlier and denying heart truth, as I was afraid to take responsibility. The beautiful part is, I am grateful, as two beautiful souls came into the world, we shared many great years together. He is a beautiful soul, who changed my life for the better. Our children are our gifts and being gifted with children changed my entire perspective on life, and the meaning of unconditional love.

It is vital to grieve, acknowledge the sadness, the loss, and express the anger. Ask and know when to be held by those who support your journey. Many times, it is the Angelic Realm that are assisting this process of support and inner healing, and often it is the Pleiadeans and other Extra-terrestrial beings. As I write these final editions, the Light Beings are supporting the Ascension process and upgrading of energies that are happening, this moment here on planet earth.

Trauma must be released, and while timing is important, only the individual will know when it is time to let it go. The letting go should be facilitated by those who know how to create the essential safe space and have a deep understanding of trauma and its multi-faced impact. The nervous system can never be forced and must be facilitated with expert guidance and loving kindness; imagine it being like the delicate petals of the flower, when the sunshine glows upon it, it opens all its free will.

Old views on sensuality have shifted and shifting. I am here to lead the way into a new way of seeing and being, from Soul remembrance of embodiment of wisdom. This is revealed more within the journey to rise as the blossoming Wildflower – Reclaiming a Sacred Place. There was a transition of mustering the courage to honour my heart and soul calling, at that moment in time. I am still navigating and fine tuning this soul direction leaping into the unknown, as some may feel I will have flipped the other way. Consciousness shifts and the life-force energy must flow freely, with no chains and no limitations of the mind.

Much is revealed within the ancient wisdom, principles and keys of the Soul Codes – Remembering Your Mission. To say all is revealed would be untrue as the vibration field of awareness is ever-expanding, changing and upgrading.

It is not what happens, it is the meaning we give it.

It is your choice when to Break-Free and allow Your Soul to Breathe.

Infinite blessings of Love-light and Light-love,

May the truth be the cornerstone to your own soul adventure.

"I wonder where life will take us..."

BIBLIOGRAPHICAL RESOURCES

Books are tools to inspire, touch and show another way of moving forward. They may talk of the science or the philosophy, and sooner or later the reader absorbs what is required for their own soul remembrance. To integrate the knowledge with daily disciplined action shifts into wisdom. It is wisdom that will deepen the connection to the heart and for each soul to remember their soul mission.

We each have a powerful mission. Allow the books to choose you, as we each have different paths to follow and express freely.

"The Science of" trilogy, by Wallace D. Wattles

– The Science of Getting Rich (1910)

– The Science of Being Great (1910)

– The Science of Being Well (1910)

The Master Key System (1912), by Charles F. Haanel

You Can Heal Your Life (1984), by Louise L. Hay

Eastern Body, Western Mind: Psychology and the Chakra System as a Path to the Self (2004), by Anodea Judith

The Vortex: Where the Law of Attraction Assembles All Cooperative Relationships (2009), by Esther and Jerry Hicks

Acknowledgments

Firstly, to my children who chose me as their Mum to guide on this first part of their lives. Jake and Charlie, you inspire me to be the greatest version of myself. I love you eternally, we have danced in many lifetimes together, and this book is dedicated to you both. No matter what happens, 'Never give up on you!' and stand proud in who you choose to be. It is not what happens to us, it is the meaning we give it. Your past does not define you, if anyone calls you weird, take it as a compliment.

To my family, Mum and Sister, thank you for catching me when I fell and being a part of this winding road. The best was yet to present and I am embracing it all! You both have inspired me in my growing into adulthood. I Love you all, the Evans, Bell and Keeley families.

To Geoff, the father of our children, and who has continued to be a rock of support as I have pursued my soul calling. Thank you for co-parenting our sons. You are a great man with a generous heart.

To my Divine Soul Sister and Editor Mel Keith, for your friendship, raw honesty and a Soul that truly gets all aspects of Zoe. A rare breed and pure diamond who with her patience, time and expertise brought my memoir into a digestible read whilst maintaining the pure essence of my story.

To Georgina, thank you for our friendship and the brilliant idea of word smithing the foreword and a way to infuse those that know my true essence into this book series. We are two peas in a pod SiStar.

To all Soul brothers and Soul sisters, global connections, thank you for being lights of inspiration and at times reflective resistance in my life. May you understand why I see life the way I do and may this create a positive change in our local communities and for team humanity. Please pay the book forward to those who are still stuck in their pain. It is time for us all to find a way to be free.

Thank you, YOUniverse for hearing my call. To bring the perfect teachers, human experiences into my life, to walk the path of healing, transformation and awakening my soul remembrance and global mission.

Thank you, Soul, for never giving up on finding a way.

ABOUT THE AUTHOR

Zoe-Anna Bell is a Relationship Guide, Author, International Healer and Trauma Healing Facilitator. She works globally with adults and teenagers.

Zoe-Anna lives in Sydney with her two children and spends her days writing, sharing poetry and holding space for healing. A Mission for Team Humanity.

"The journey of the Soul is the doorway to love"

She is available for podcasts, hosting retreats and speaking engagements. There is much healing to be done.

CONNECT WITH ZOE

Looking to stay connected? I'd like to support you through your journey, and value feedback. Feel free to explore my community.

Business website www.zoe-anna.com

Email contact: info@zoe-anna.com

Business Network: linkedin.com/in/zoe-anna-bell/

Social Media pages: instagram.com/zoeanna_bell

As an author, Zoe has published these books:

- The Adventures of Pinky Fairway – A Journey to Awaken Your Spirit and Set Yourself Free (2017), Zoe Bell
- Raw – A Key to A Woman's Heart and Soul (2017), Zoe Bell
- Completeness – A Doorway to Love (2018), Zoe Bell
- Free Wildflower Codes – book trilogy (2021), Zoe Bell

Co-authoring

- Healing Prolapse – (2021) Shannon Dunn.
  A contributing chapter on the Divine Masculine & Feminine.

COMPLETION OF THE STORY

NOW A BLANK SLATE

12th August 2021

www.ingramcontent.com/pod-product-compliance
Lightning Source LLC
Chambersburg PA
CBHW050307010526
44107CB00055B/2138